SHENANDOAH NATIONAL PARK, BLUE RIDGE PARKWAY,

AND

GREAT SMOKY MOUNTAINS NATIONAL PARK

A FIELD GUIDE

by
Ernest Preston Edwards

Principal Illustrator
Edward Murrell Butler

with other illustrations by
Ramiel Papish and F. P. Bennett

The McDonald and Woodward Publishing Company
Blacksburg, Virginia

The McDonald & Woodward Publishing Company
Blacksburg, Virginia, and Granville, Ohio
www.mwpubco.com

*Birds of Shenandoah National Park, Blue Ridge Parkway,
and Great Smoky Mountains National Park: A Field Guide*

Copyright © 2006 by Ernest Preston Edwards.
All rights reserved. First printing March 2006.
Printed in Canada by Friesens, Altona, Manitoba.

15 14 13 12 10 09 08 07 06   10 9 8 7 6 5 4 3 2 1

Library of Congress Cataloging-in-Publication Data

Birds of Shenandoah National Park, Blue Ridge Parkway, and
Great Smoky Mountains National Park: a field guide / Ernest
Preston Edwards, principal illustrator. . . [et al.].
     p. cm.
   Includes index.
   ISBN 0-939923-96-3 (alk. paper)
  1. Birds--Virginia--Shenandoah National Park--Identification.
2. Birds--Blue Ridge Parkway (N.C. and Va.)--Identification.
3. Birds--Great Smoky Mountains National Park (N.C. and
Tenn.)--Identification. 1. Edwards, Ernest Preston, 1919-
   QL684,V8B575 2006
   598.09755--dc22

                                            2006001300

BIRDS

OF

SHENANDOAH NATIONAL PARK, BLUE RIDGE PARKWAY, AND GREAT SMOKY MOUNTAINS NATIONAL PARK

A FIELD GUIDE

Contents

Dedicated
to the memory of my wife

Mabel Thacher Edwards

and to

Mrs. Myriam P. Moore,
the Lynchburg Bird Club,
and
the Virginia Society of Ornithology

Preface

The great surge of popular interest in birds in recent years has been accompanied by a corresponding increase in the number of bird-related publications. For those persons mainly interested in identifying birds near their home or within a relatively small geographic area, however, this expanding list of literature represents something of a paradox. While there are more and more checklists, breeding bird atlases, and bird-*finding* guidebooks focused specifically on one state, one region, or even one county, bird-*identification* guidebooks have seemed to trend toward larger size, to incorporate larger areas, and to devote more and more text and illustrations to the identification of species which the average bird watcher (or professional ornithologist, for that matter) might never see or hear in a lifetime. By comparison, common but sometimes puzzling species which anyone might see fairly often in his or her own backyard, or in a nearby nature center or city park, often seem to be given relatively less attention.

My small book, however, *does* concern itself with the *identification* of birds — birds that occur in a relatively small part of the Appalachian Mountains. The region I have chosen to cover in this book includes the areas within and near Shenandoah National Park, Blue Ridge Parkway, and Great Smoky Mountains National Park. Specifically, the area of coverage includes the terrain and localities within a distance of approximately twenty miles on either side of Shenandoah National Park's Skyline Drive (SD) and Blue

Ridge Parkway (BRP), and the terrain and localities within approximately five miles of Great Smoky Mountains National Park (GSMNP). This area incorporates much of the Blue Ridge Physiographic Province that occurs in the states of North Carolina, Tennessee, and Virginia. I hope that this book will provide the people living in or visiting this region a fully illustrated, useful, convenient, and lightweight reference that will help them identify and otherwise better appreciate the birds they might encounter in this beautiful and biologically rich land.

Acknowledgments

I appreciate very much the many pages of bird images provided by Edward Murrell Butler, the Principal Illustrator, which were first published in *A Field Guide to the Birds of Mexico and Adjacent Areas,* published by The University of Texas Press in 1998. I thank the University of Texas Press for granting permission for the use of images for 226 species. Also I am greatly indebted to Ramiel Papish for providing images for forty-seven species, and F. P. Bennett for providing the illustrations for three species of terns. The author prepared images for twenty-one species.

The text for this book could not have been nearly as well organized, authoritative, and up-to-date without the careful and perceptive edits of the manuscript by Thelma Dalmas, Teta Kain, Harry LeGrand, Jr., and Eugene Sattler. I appreciate very much their help and their patience in working with me on this project.

Also deserving great credit are the hundreds of members of the Virginia Society of Ornithology, the Carolina Bird Club, and the Tennessee Ornithological Society, and the various local bird clubs in and near our area, who have spent thousands of hours in the field and have reported their findings to the appropriate bird records committees, checklist committees, rare bird alerts, publications committees, hawk watch groups, Christmas bird count groups, etc. Working independently or together, they have built up a great body of knowledge of the birds of the area. I also want to recognize YuLee Larner, who chaired the committee which produced the first edition of *Virginia's Birdlife* in 1979, and did much of the work on the second edition, published in 1987. I thank her, her committee, and their counterparts in other state and local clubs and societies who provided information that has been useful to me in the preparation of this book.

Lastly, I want to thank Nancy Haack of the National Park Service for providing maps that were used as bases for the figures that appear on pages 5 through 7 below.

Ernest Preston Edwards,
February 17, 2005

Introduction

The Blue Ridge and Great Smoky Mountains have been of great interest to naturalists for many years. The peaks and ridges, the steep or gentle mountain slopes, and the intervening valleys and flatlands provide a multitude of habitats which, in turn, support the area's great diversity of plant and animal life. The bird life of the region is rich, ecologically diverse, and biogeographically intriguing. Birds of generally more southerly distribution nest at lower elevations while those of generally more northerly distribution nest on the upper slopes and ridges, both groups often on the same mountain. Adding to the diversity of birds in the fall, winter, and spring are those species which nest even farther north but migrate into or through our area during those seasons. Altogether, some 336 species representing 58 families and 19 orders either breed in or travel to or through this region, a fact that affords birders and naturalists abundant opportunity to view, study, and enjoy this resource.

As human populations in and near our area have grown, and the area has become more and more accessible and attractive to the general public, many guidebooks, magazine articles, and other descriptive materials have been produced about the natural and cultural heritage of the Blue Ridge and Great Smoky Mountains — about hiking, biking, camping, driving back roads, visiting historic places, sampling local crafts and participating in festivals, and looking for wildflowers. The birds of the region, of course, have not been overlooked, but here, as elsewhere, these publications have devoted very little attention specifically to bird *identification*. To remedy this situation, I have created this book as a practical and convenient resource to help readers more easily, rapidly, and confidently identify the birds that they might encounter in and near our area.

Much information about how to find and identify birds in general is available in the numerous field guides now on the market, and consequently I make no effort to repeat that information here. Some notes about the organization and use of this field guide, however, are included.

1. The greater part of this book is devoted to those species of birds that occur regularly in the Great Smoky Mountains and the Blue Ridge of North Carolina and Virginia. For each of these species, I provide a brief description of adults, their habitat preferences, and their status as resident or transient. Other descriptive or geographic notes are provided when appropriate. At least one image of each species is presented on the page facing the description; these images are in color for all but fifteen species.

2. The kinds of birds which are not to be expected on most field trips but nonetheless might be seen a few times every ten or twenty years, or are extremely rare or localized in distribution, or might accidentally stray into our area are treated in a special section at the back of the book. This arrangement has been done to help reduce any confusion that these species might create with the identification of regularly occurring species described in the main body of the book.

3. If a species occurs throughout our area, no mention of its range is made in the species descriptions. However, if a species is absent from one part of the area, we list, at the end of the species description, the part or parts of the region — Shenandoah National Park and its primary north-south roadway, the Skyline Drive (SD); Blue

Ridge Parkway (BRP); or Great Smoky Mountains National Park (GSMNP) — in which it *does* occur.

4. The greater part of the book is taken up by two major groups of birds — Water Birds (waders and swimmers) and Land Birds (birds of fields, yards, and forests). Land Birds are further divided into two groups, the more primitive land birds (such as game birds, hawks, owls, woodpeckers, etc.) and the more advanced land birds (such as flycatchers, vireos, crows, thrushes, warblers, sparrows, blackbirds, etc.). The illustrations of birds in each of the three resulting groups are color coded with the use of a vertical stripe along the right side of the page — a blue stripe signifies water birds, a gold stripe signifies primitive land birds that are primarily active during daytime, a reddish-brown stripe signifies primitive land birds that are primarily active at night, and a green stripe signifies advanced land birds. *Within* each of the three groups, the birds are arranged in taxonomic sequence.

Naturally there is an imperfect fit among some taxonomic groups placed in Water Birds and Land Birds. In such cases, I have left each species in the group that includes most of its close relatives. For example, the Osprey and the Kingfisher are left with Land Birds while the Upland Sandpiper and the American Woodcock are left with Water Birds.

5. In the case of the night birds and a few other species with very distinctive, easily described songs or calls, I have included in the descriptions a short note about the voice. It has been my experience that descriptions of songs are mainly useful as a reminder of songs you have previously learned from a sound recording or by hearing a known bird singing.

6. Generalized maps of Shenandoah National Park, Blue Ridge Parkway, and Great Smoky Mountains National Park appear on pages 5 to 7. These maps provide small-

scale representation of the more than six hundred miles of parkland from northern Virginia to southwestern North Carolina and southeastern Tennessee that are covered in this book. In addition to the featured roadways within the three national park areas, the maps show major highways and selected towns and cities near the parks, all of which will help the reader become oriented with the different parts of the region. Of particular importance are the numerous visitor centers within or adjacent to the parks; selected visitor centers are identified with a star (★) on the maps and these, along with others in the area, will be good sources of helpful information for users of this book.

This book covers much of the area shown on figures 1, 2, and 3.

7. A checklist of birds of our area is included near the end of the book. This checklist is arranged in taxonomic sequence, first by order, then by family and species, and it includes all of the kinds of birds which, to my knowledge, have been reported in the area.

8. A standard alphabetic index of birds mentioned in the text is included at the end of the book.

Recommended Resources

The bird-*finding* guidebook specifically designed and written to cover the best localities for birding in the Blue Ridge, and the one I highly recommend for use along with my book, is *Birds of the Blue Ridge Mountains* by Marcus B. Simpson, Jr., published by the University of North Carolina Press.

Three other guidebooks which cover parts of our area are *A Birder's Guide to Virginia,* compiled by David W. Johnston and published by the American Birding Association; *Birds of Shenandoah National Park: A Naturalist's View,* written by Terry and Patressa Lindsay and published

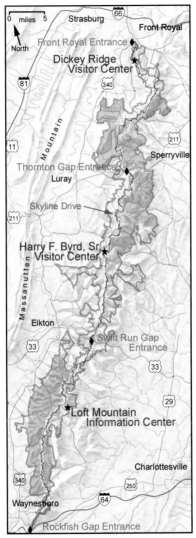

Figure 1. Shenandoah National Park lies astride the Blue Ridge in northern Virginia. The Skyline Drive, shown here in red, runs the entire length of the park, a distance of 105 miles.

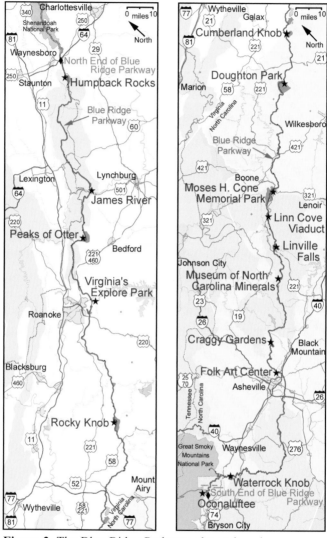

Figure 2. The Blue Ridge Parkway, shown here in green, extends some 465 miles between Shenandoah National Park in Virginia and Great Smoky Mountains National Park in North Carolina. The northern part of the parkway is shown at left and the southern part is shown at right.

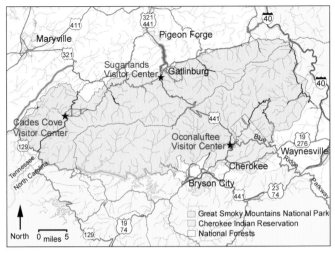

Figure 3. Great Smoky Mountains National Park lies within the Great Smoky Mountains of North Carolina and Tennessee.

Notes relative to the maps

by the Shenandoah National Park Association; and *Birds of the Smokies,* written by Fred J. Alsop, III, published by Great Smoky Mountains Natural History Association. All three of these titles are very useful in their respective areas of coverage.

Recordings of bird songs on CDs or cassettes also should be helpful. Among those available for our area are *Guide to Bird Songs* (National Geographic Society and Cornell Laboratory of Ornithology), *Stokes Field Guide to Bird Song (Eastern),* and *Eastern/Central Bird Songs* in the Peterson Field Guides series.

The numerous informational publications found at visitor centers located along the roads in and near the Blue Ridge and Great Smoky Mountains should not be overlooked. Many of these, especially the maps, can be very useful.

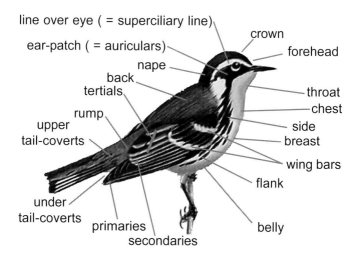

Figure 4. Parts of a bird.

Abbreviations, Symbols, and Words with Specific Meanings Used in Species Descriptions

3.5", etc. = length of bird from bill tip to tail tip

• = seasonal status and preferred habitats

♂ = male

♀ = female

above (as in "barred above") = upper surface

ad = adult

below (as in "barred below") = lower surface

BRP = Blue Ridge Parkway

f = female (adult, if not modified)

GSMNP = Great Smoky Mountains National Park

Id = notes on identification

im = immature

m = male (adult, if not modified)

resident = lives in the area for the specified time

SD = Shenandoah National Park's Skyline Drive

sum = summer

transient = migrates through our area

<u>V</u> = voice, song, or call

win = winter

NC = North Carolina

VA = Virginia

Geese, Swans, and Ducks — Anatidae

Snow Goose
Chen caerulescens

Id: 28"; wing-tips black; **white morph ad:** mostly white; pinkish legs and bill; **white morph im:** pale gray above; bill and legs black; **dark morph ad:** white head and upper neck; dark gray back and belly; pale wing-patch; **dark morph im:** mostly blackish-gray, with black bill and legs; tail coverts white.
   • Rare transient and winter visitor; wet fields, marshes, lakes.

Canada Goose
Branta canadensis

Id: 35–45"; black neck and head, except white "strap" under throat; upper tail-coverts form a white "U" on top of black tail; underparts paler or darker. See also **Cackling Goose** — p. 124.
   • Year-round resident; lakes, ponds, in marshes, grassy areas.

Tundra Swan
Cygnus columbianus

Id: 52"; very long neck; **ad:** all-white (including flight-feathers), except black bill and feet, and (usually) small yellow base-of-bill spot; **im:** pale gray, lighter below; bill grayish pink, blackish-tipped. V: a melodious *whoo*.
   • SD and VA BRP. Rare transient and winter visitor; large lakes, marshes.

Wood Duck
Aix sponsa

Id: 18"; floppy nape-crest; **m:** white and black face, glossed green and purple; neck and breast chestnut; **f:** streaked below; head gray with white tear-drop-shaped eye-patch.
   • Year-round resident; lakes, ponds, swamps.

Gadwall
Anas strepera

Id: 20"; reddish brown wing-patch; speculum white; **m:** breast and sides finely mottled gray; head brownish; under and upper tail-coverts black; **f:** mottled brown; paler head.
   • SD and BRP. Transient and winter visitor; lakes, ponds.

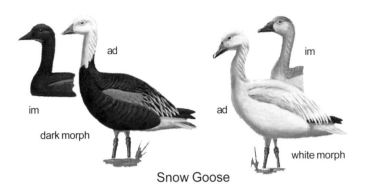

Snow Goose

Tundra Swan

Canada Goose

Wood Duck

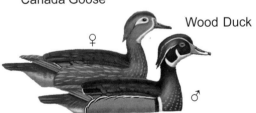

Gadwall

11

American Wigeon   *Anas americana*

Id: 20"; **m:** has white wing-patch and crown; and green eye-patch; and **f:** wing-patch whitish; head grayish, finely streaked; sides *not* heavily mottled; breast tinged dull reddish brown.
   • Transient and winter visitor; lakes, marshes.

American Black Duck   *Anas rubripes*

Id: 23"; both sexes are like female Mallard, but female Black Duck is darker, and male is *much* darker; and the purple (*not* blue) speculum *is not* white-bordered; and the female Black Duck's bill is dull greenish-yellow, *not* dull orange and blackish brown.
   • Transient, winter visitor, and rare summer resident; ponds, lakes, marshes.

Mallard   *Anas platyrhynchos*

Id: 24"; tail white; **m:** green head, white collar, yellow bill; **f:** mottled yellowish brown; bill yellowish orange and dull dark brown or blackish; speculum white-bordered on leading and trailing edge; lateral tail feathers mostly white.
   • Year-round resident; ponds, lakes, marshes.

Blue-winged Teal   *Anas discors*

Id: 16"; green speculum; large blue wing-patch (may be almost hidden); **m:** head dark blue, with white crescent; **f:** mottled grayish brown.
   • Transient, and very rare summer visitor; lakes, marshes.

Northern Shoveler   *Anas clypeata*

Id: 18"; bill dark, heavy, very broad near tip; large blue wing-patch; **m:** green head, white breast, reddish brown flanks; **f:** mottled yellowish brown; see female teals.
   • Rare transient and winter visitor; ponds, lakes, marshes.

Northern Pintail   *Anas acuta*

Id: 28", 22"; long neck, long tail; **m:** brown head; neck mostly white; **f:** mottled.
   • Rare transient and winter visitor; lakes, marshes.

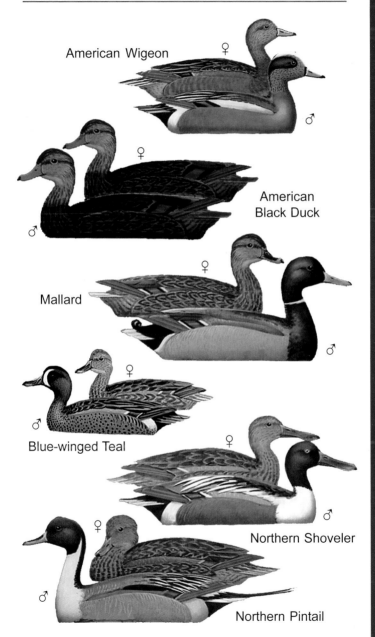

American Wigeon ♀ ♂

American Black Duck ♀ ♂

Mallard ♀ ♂

Blue-winged Teal ♀ ♂

Northern Shoveler ♀ ♂

Northern Pintail ♀ ♂

Green-winged Teal   *Anas crecca*

Id: 14"; **m:** dark reddish brown head, with very large green eye-patch; spotted breast; gray sides; **f:** streaked and mottled; green speculum; *no* blue patch on wing.
• Rare transient and winter visitor; lakes, ponds, marshes.

Canvasback   *Aythya valisineria*

Id: 22"; like Redhead, but forehead slopes into long, black, heavy-based bill; **m:** red of head darker and browner, back and sides whiter; **f:** head and neck pale brown; back and sides pale gray.
• SD and BRP. Rare transient and winter visitor; large lakes, rivers.

Redhead   *Aythya americana*

Id: 21"; bill short, with white bar near tip, does *not* slope into forehead; **m:** reddish brown head; black breast; sides and back pale gray; **f:** mostly brownish; with some white on face. See Ring-necked Duck and Canvasback.
• SD and BRP. Rare transient and winter visitor; lakes.

Ring-necked Duck   *Aythya collaris*

Id: 19"; white bar near tip of bill; **m:** back black; **f:** darker than Redhead; area around base of bill whitish, but *not* contrasty. See Lesser Scaup.
• Transient and winter visitor; lakes.

Greater Scaup   *Aythya marila*

Id: 19"; long white wing-stripe shows in flight; **m:** head, neck, and breast black; green gloss on head; **f:** darker than Redhead; like Lesser Scaup, except wing-stripe. See Lesser Scaup.
• SD and BRP. Rare transient and winter visitor; lakes.

Lesser Scaup   *Aythya affinis*

Id: 17"; short white wing-stripe shows in flight; no white bar on bill; **m:** usually purplish gloss on head; much paler on back (gray) than Ring-necked Duck (black); **f:** dark brown; contrasty white area around base of bill.
• Transient and winter visitor; lakes, ponds.

Green-winged Teal

Canvasback

Redhead

Ring-necked Duck

Greater Scaup

Lesser Scaup

15

Bufflehead
Bucephala albeola

Id: 14"; head appears puffy, high-crowned; **m:** white below, black and white above; much of head behind eye white, the rest mostly glossy black; **f:** whitish below; blackish-brown back and head; white patch behind eye.

• Transient and winter visitor; lakes.

Common Goldeneye
Bucephala clangula

Id: 21"; head appears puffy, high-crowned; bill short, dark; **m:** white below; black and white above; head dark green; rounded white patch between eye and bill; **f:** grayish above and below; with white collar; head all dark brown. See Bufflehead and Common Merganser.

• Transient and winter visitor; lakes.

Hooded Merganser
Lophodytes cucullatus

Id: 18"; slender, black bill; **m:** black and white head-and-breast pattern; fan-shaped crest; tawny sides; **f:** brown head; smaller crest dull tawny. See Bufflehead.

• Transient and winter visitor, rare in summer; lakes, ponds, rivers.

Common Merganser
Mergus merganser

Id: 25"; **m:** head and upper neck black, green-glossed; lower neck, breast, and sides white; bill slender, red; large white wing-patch; **f:** head (except white throat) and upper neck rufous; in contrast to white lower neck and breast; small white wing-patch.

• Rare transient and winter visitor; deep ponds, large lakes.

Red-breasted Merganser
Mergus serrator

Id: 23"; like Common Merganser, but has much shaggier crest; **m:** breast dull reddish brown with spotty blackish streaks; grayish sides and flanks; **f:** sides of neck, and fore-neck, whitish, *not* in marked contrast to whitish breast and throat.

• Transient and rare winter visitor; lakes, rivers.

Ruddy Duck
Oxyura jamaicensis

Id: 16"; **sum m:** reddish brown; with black and white head; blue bill; **win m:** grayish brown; head dark brown and white, less contrasty; bill dull bluish gray; **f:** grayish brown above; much paler below; one dark stripe on whitish face.

• Transient, and rare winter visitor; lakes, ponds.

Bufflehead   Common Goldeneye

Hooded Merganser

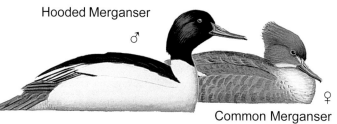

Common Merganser

Red-breasted Merganser

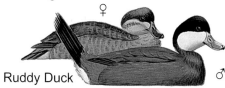

Ruddy Duck

Loons — Gaviidae

Common Loon   *Gavia immer*

   Id: 33"; bill heavy, straight, dark; **win:** plumage gray above, whitish below; sides of face and neck grayish, slightly blotchy; *no* back-speckles; **sum:** rows of large white spots above; head and neck black with greenish gloss; two partial, striped collars.
   • Transient, and winter resident; large lakes, rivers.

Grebes — Podicipedidae

Pied-billed Grebe   *Podilymbus podiceps*

   Id: 13"; mostly dark grayish brown, with whitish belly and under tail-coverts; bill short, stout, pale; **win:** throat white; bill plain; **sum:** throat, and ring on bill, black .
   • Transient, and winter resident, rare summer resident; marshy ponds, lakes, slow-moving rivers.

Horned Grebe   *Podiceps auritus*

   Id: 13"; blackish gray above; bill short, slender; iris red; **win:** ear-patch all-white; and hind-neck and fore-neck contrasty blackish and white; **sum:** neck chestnut; neat tawny face-plumes extend backward, mostly above eye.
   • Transient, winter, and rare summer resident; ponds, lakes.

Cormorants — Phalacrocoracidae

Double-crested Cormorant   *Phalacrocorax auritus*

   Id: 32"; **ad:** black, with dark green sheen; *rounded* orange-yellow throat-pouch; **im:** dark brown above and below, except whitish throat and breast; throat-pouch yellow.
   • Transient; also summer and winter visitor near SD and VA BRP.

sum

win

Common Loon

sum

win

sum

win

Pied-billed Grebe

Horned Grebe

sum

im

Double-crested Cormorant

All images on this page are black-and-white.

Bitterns, Herons, Egrets, and Night-Herons
— Ardeidae

American Bittern   *Botaurus lentiginosus*

Id: 26"; general yellowish brown to reddish brown plumage; with a broad black streak on side of face and upper neck; heavy spotty streaks of dark reddish brown on neck, breast and back. <u>V</u>: a loud *chunk-uh-lunk.*

• Transient, and rare summer resident; marshes, especially cattails, and marshy borders of ponds and lakes.

Least Bittern   *Ixobrychus exilis*

Id: 12"; rich buff wing-patches contrast with black wing-tips and tail; **m:** black back and crown; **f:** dark reddish brown back and crown. When flushed it flies farther, and with slower wing-beats, than rails.

• Rare transient and summer resident; marshes, marshy borders of ponds and lakes.

Great Blue Heron   *Ardea herodias*

Id: 45"; medium bluish gray above; head whitish, with slender black plumes behind eye; dull buffy gray to black below; much larger than any other heron in the area, except the all-white-plumaged Great Egret.

• Year-round resident; marshes, swampy or marshy borders of lakes, ponds, rivers.

Great Egret   *Ardea alba*

Id: 38"; plumage all-white; bill yellow; feet and legs blackish.

• Rare transient and late-summer visitor; marshes, lakes, ponds.

Snowy Egret   *Egretta thula*

Id: 22"; like immature Little Blue Heron, but has black bill; black legs (or front of legs blackish and back of legs yellowish); and yellow or yellow-orange, *not* dark greenish, feet (toes).

• SD and BRP. Rare transient and late-summer visitor; marshes, swampy areas, ponds.

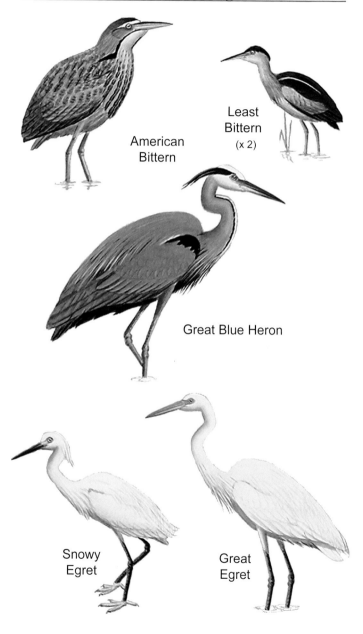

American
Bittern

Least
Bittern
(x 2)

Great Blue Heron

Snowy
Egret

Great
Egret

Little Blue Heron   *Egretta caerulea*

Id: 25"; bill bluish gray, broadly black-tipped; **ad:** slaty blue, with greenish to blackish legs; purplish neck and head; **im:** white, or mottled white and blue, legs and feet dull greenish.

• Rare late-summer visitor; marshes, ponds, lakes.

Tricolored Heron   *Egretta tricolor*

Id: 24"; bill long, slender; underparts and stripe down front of neck, white; neck and upperparts mostly dark blue; **im:** wings mottled with reddish brown; neck mostly dull tawny brown.

• SD and BRP. Rare transient and late-summer visitor; marshes, shores of lakes and ponds.

Cattle Egret   *Bubulcus ibis*

Id: 24"; rather short, stout, yellow to red-orange bill; legs dark greenish to yellowish to orange-red; breeding birds have tawny-buff plumes on crown, chest, and back.

• SD and BRP. Rare transient and summer visitor; usually seen with livestock in moist to wet grassy fields.

Green Heron   *Butorides virescens*

Id: 16"; **ad:** gray and dark green above; sides of neck reddish brown; legs yellow to orange; **im:** duller; streaked dark brown and white on sides of neck and underparts.

• Transient, summer resident, and very rare winter visitor; swamps, marshes, ponds, river banks.

Black-crowned Night-Heron   *Nycticorax nycticorax*

Id: 26"; head relatively large; **ad:** back black; wings light gray; underparts white; **im:** brown above, with prominent pale spots; heavily streaked brown and buff below.

• Rare year-round; swamps, marshes, ponds.

Yellow-crowned Night-Heron   *Nyctanassa violacea*

Id: 26"; head relatively large; **ad:** medium to dark gray body and wings; back streaked; head black-and-white, with tawny to yellowish plumed crown; **im:** streaked and mottled; slightly grayer above, and has smaller spots, than immature Black-crowned Night-Heron.

• Rare transient and localized summer resident; swamps, marshes, ponds.

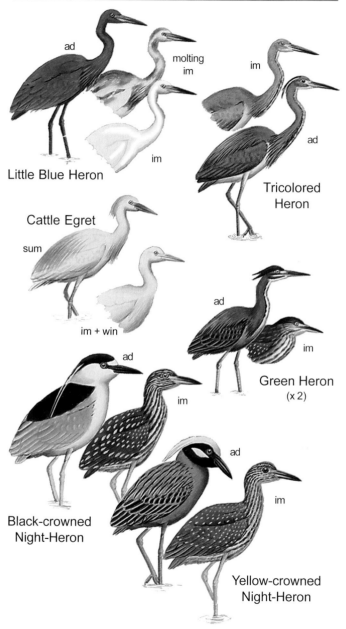

Little Blue Heron

ad

molting im

im

Tricolored Heron

im

ad

Cattle Egret

sum

im + win

Green Heron
(x 2)

ad

im

Black-crowned
Night-Heron

ad

im

Yellow-crowned
Night-Heron

ad

im

23

Ibises — Threskiornithidae

White Ibis   *Eudocimus albus*

   Id: 23"; long legs and long decurved bill reddish; **ad:** white, with black wing-tips; **im:** white below; brown above (may be mottled); head and neck streaked.

   • SD and BRP. Rare and localized year-round visitor; marshes, ponds, wet meadows, lakes.

Rails and Coots — Rallidae

King Rail   *Rallus elegans*

   Id: 16"; heavy black streaks on tawny olive above; wing-coverts and fore-neck and breast rufous; flanks and under tail-coverts barred black and white; bill stout and long.

   • SD and BRP. Rare transient and localized summer resident; marshes, marshy shores of ponds and lakes.

Virginia Rail   *Rallus limicola*

   Id: 8"; **ad:** like King Rail, but much smaller; sides of face grayer; **im:** darker, with heavy blurred blackish streaks on throat and breast.

   • SD and BRP. Rare transient and localized summer resident; marshes, marshy borders of ponds, lakes, sluggish rivers.

Sora   *Porzana carolina*

   Id: 8"; **ad:** grayish brown above, streaked; pale gray below, with black throat to chest; flanks whitish-barred; **im:** duller; has brownish wash; throat *not* black.

   • SD and BRP. Rare transient and localized year-round resident or visitor; numbers decreasing; marshes, marshy shores of ponds, lakes, sluggish rivers.

American Coot   *Fulica americana*

   Id: 15"; **ad:** mostly blackish gray; bill white; **im:** paler; bill whitish.

   • Transient, local winter resident, and rare summer visitor; ponds, lakes, marshes; often walks on open shores.

White Ibis
(x 0.75)

ad

im

King Rail

im

ad

Virginia Rail

im

Sora

ad

American Coot

25

Plovers — Charadriidae

Black-bellied Plover   *Pluvialis squatarola*

Id: 12"; **win:** mottled gray above; black patch under wing (shows in flight), pale gray below, faintly streaked; large head; thick black bill; black legs; **sum:** more contrasty above; black face and underparts; but belly and under tail-coverts white.

• SD and BRP. Rare transient; lake shores, wet fields.

American Golden-Plover   *Pluvialis dominica*

Id: 11"; like Black-bellied Plover, but more yellowish above; **win:** buffier below; no black patch under wing; **sum:** mostly black (*not* white) lower belly and under tail-coverts.

• Rare transient; grassy fields, mud flats, marshes.

Semipalmated Plover   *Charadrius semipalmatus*

Id: 7"; medium brown above; forehead, throat, collar, and most of underparts white; legs orange; **sum:** black fore-crown, eye-patch, and breast-band; bill orange with black tip; **win:** crown, eye patch, and breast band brown; bill dark.

• Transient; mud flats, sandy lake shores.

Killdeer   *Charadrius vociferus*

Id: 11"; brown above; white forehead, throat, collar, and most of underparts; two black breast-bands, the upper one forming a full collar; rump, upper tail-coverts, and much of tail salmon-colored; bill black. V̲: a loud, high-pitched, somewhat squeaky *kil-dee*, a musical *dee-it* and *dee-dee-dee-dee*

• Year-round resident; wet fields, farmland, open shores of ponds or lakes.

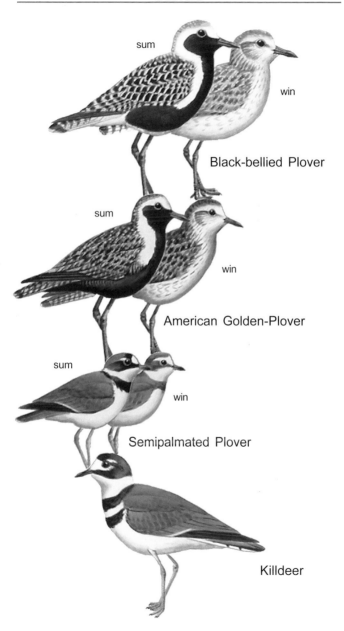

sum

win

Black-bellied Plover

sum

win

American Golden-Plover

sum

win

Semipalmated Plover

Killdeer

Sandpipers — Scolopacidae

Greater Yellowlegs   *Tringa melanoleuca*

Id: 14"; mottled gray above; white below with many fine neck-streaks; spots and bars on sides; bill long, black, very slightly up-curved; upper tail-coverts white. <u>V</u>: a loud, *three*-noted *hew-hew-hew*. See Lesser Yellowlegs.
  • Transient; mud flats, ponds, marshy fields, lake shores.

Lesser Yellowlegs   *Tringa flavipes*

Id: 11"; like Greater Yellowlegs, but smaller; bill shorter, straighter; usually not as heavily marked on neck, chest, and sides. <u>V</u>: one or two whistled notes.
  • Transient; mud flats, lake shores, marshes, ponds.

Solitary Sandpiper   *Tringa solitaria*

Id: 8"; speckled whitish on dark grayish brown above, with white eye-ring; neck and chest finely streaked; legs dull greenish, *not* yellow; much white on outer tail feathers.
  • Transient; mud flats, ponds, stream banks.

Willet   *Catoptrophorus semipalmatus*

Id: 15"; striking black-and-white wing-patch in flight; bill long, straight, rather heavy; **win:** mostly unstreaked gray neck and upperparts; unstreaked whitish below; **sum:** mottled and streaked gray above; streaked neck and breast.
  • Very rare transient; lake shores, mud flats.

Spotted Sandpiper   *Actitis macularius*

Id: 7"; **win:** gray above; unspotted white below; bill dark; and **sum:** heavy black spots below; bill orange, black-tipped; legs yellowish. Flies with stiff, rapid, shallow wing-beats, showing white wing-stripe; when walking it pumps its body up and down.
  • Transient, and rare and erratic summer resident; shores of ponds, lakes, streams, rivers.

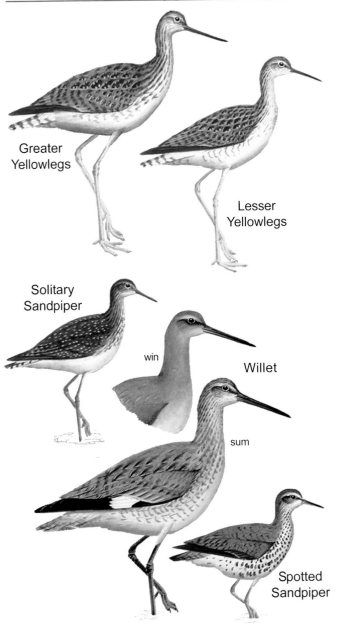

Greater Yellowlegs

Lesser Yellowlegs

Solitary Sandpiper

win

Willet

sum

Spotted Sandpiper

29

Upland Sandpiper   *Bartramia longicauda*

Id: 12"; mottled light and dark grayish brown above; neck buffy, finely streaked; chest and sides lightly streaked to barred; long legs dull yellowish; bill rather short, straight, mostly dark. V: a *wheet-wheeo* "wolf-whistle" and a *wheer-wheer.*

• SD and BRP. Rare transient (and very rare summer resident in the VA portion of our area); in extensive open grassland, moist fields, open grassy marshes.

Ruddy Turnstone   *Arenaria interpres*

Id: 9"; black-and-white wing, tail, rump, and belly pattern, in all seasons; bill short, black; legs orange; **win:** mottled very dark brownish gray above; pale grayish patch on sides of blackish chest; with a trace of summer head pattern; **sum:** black-and-white head and neck; bright rufous-and-black wings and back.

• SD and VA BRP. Rare transient; lake shores, mud flats.

Sanderling   *Calidris alba*

Id: 7"; legs black; bill medium length, black; white wing-stripe; blackish "shoulder" patch (may be hidden); **win:** whiter, less streaked than other "peeps"; underparts pure white; back pale gray, faintly streaked; **sum:** streaked head, neck, breast and upperparts, with reddish-brown wash.

• SD and BRP. Rare transient; lake shores, mud flats.

Semipalmated Sandpiper   *Calidris pusilla*

Id: 6"; like Least Sandpiper (see below) but grayer, with black legs; breast streaks very faint or absent in winter.

• Transient; lake shores, mud flats.

Western Sandpiper   *Calidris mauri*

Id: 6"; like Least Sandpiper (see below) but grayer, with black legs, and a heavier bill drooped at tip; **win:** streaky breast patch very faint or absent; **sum:** rufous ear-patch and crown.

• SD and BRP. Rare transient; lake shores, mud flats.

Upland Sandpiper

Ruddy Turnstone

sum

win

win

Sanderling

sum

sum

win

Semipalmated
Sandpiper

sum

Western
Sandpiper

win

31

Least Sandpiper   *Calidris minutilla*

Id: 6"; legs dull yellowish; bill short, slender; **win:** mottled pale and dark brownish gray above; white below, with finely streaked brownish chest-band; **sum:** mottled and streaked black and brownish gray above; and on neck and chest.
• Transient; mud flats, lake shores.

White-rumped Sandpiper   *Calidris fuscicollis*

Id: 7"; rump and upper tail-coverts white; legs blackish; **win:** grayer and paler than in summer; **sum:** mottled brownish gray above; white below with streaked brownish gray breast.
• SD and BRP. Rare transient; mud flats; lake shores, marshy ponds.

Pectoral Sandpiper   *Calidris melanotos*

Id: 9"; mottled grayish brown above; belly and under tail-coverts white; breast appears dark and contrasty, with narrow black streaks on pale brown; legs dull greenish.
• SD and BRP. Transient; lake shores, marsh pools, wet grassy fields.

Dunlin   *Calidris alpina*

Id: 8"; bill medium long, decurved near tip; legs black; **win:** faintly streaked gray breast and upperparts; white belly; **sum:** mottled rufous above; whitish below with fine black breast-streaks and *large black belly-patch*.
• SD and VA BRP. Rare transient; marshes, mud flats, wet grassy fields.

Stilt Sandpiper   *Calidris himantopus*

Id: 9"; rather long, slender, black bill; long grayish green legs; small head; white upper tail-coverts; **win:** gray above, and on breast; mostly white below; **sum:** mottled dark brown; heavily streaked breast; barred belly; trace of rufous on head.
• SD and VA BRP. Rare fall transient; mud flats, lake shores, marshes.

sum

White-rumped
Sandpiper

sum

win

Least
Sandpiper

win

Pectoral
Sandpiper

win

sum

Dunlin

sum

win

Stilt Sandpiper

Buff-breasted Sandpiper   *Tryngites subruficollis*

Id: 8"; entire underparts rich buff; "scaly" black and buff mottling above; bill short, black; legs yellowish; under-wings mostly white; head small.

• VA BRP. Rare fall transient; moist grassy fields, ponds, marshes.

Short-billed Dowitcher   *Limnodromus griseus*

Id: 11"; wedge-shaped, long, white rump-and-lower-back-patch; very long bill; **win:** gray upperparts and breast; whitish belly; faint bars on flanks; **sum:** mottled black and buffy brown above; reddish brown below, except whitish belly; spots and short bars on breast, sides, and flanks; narrow black and white tail bars. <u>V</u>: a loud *chew-chew-chew*.

• SD and BRP. Rare transient; ponds, lake shores, mud flats.

Wilson's Snipe   *Gallinago delicata*

Id: 10"; bill very long; legs short; head striped; neck, back, and breast heavily streaked black and white; tail orange and black. Flies erratically (and utters a rasping *crepe* note) when flushed.

• Transient and winter resident; marshes, wet pastures, along streams.

American Woodcock   *Scolopax minor*

Id: 11"; mottled and barred and streaked brown and pale buff to whitish above, with black bar across tail near tip; uniform pale rufous to buff below; bill very long. Flies with whistling wings when flushed or in overhead courtship flight. <u>V</u>: (usually heard in courtship) similar to the rasping *peent* of the Common Nighthawk.

• Transient and year-round resident; thickets, overgrown wet fields, wooded stream-sides.

Buff-breasted Sandpiper

sum

win

Short-billed Dowitcher

Wilson's Snipe

American Woodcock

Gulls and Terns — Laridae

Laughing Gull   *Larus atricilla*

Id: 16"; *no* white on wing-tip; **sum ad:** mostly white, including tail; head all-black; bill red; dark gray back and wings; black wing-tips; **win ad:** black bill, head mostly white, with gray around eye to nape; **1st win:** dark brownish gray above, gray breast, white belly; mostly black tail (including outer tail feathers) with white tail base and upper tail-coverts.

• Rare transient; shores of lakes and ponds, flooded fields; most likely to be seen after coastal storms.

Bonaparte's Gull   *Larus philadelphia*

Id: 14"; like Laughing Gull, but **sum ad:** much paler wings and back; and broadly white wing-tips; black bill; bright red legs; and **win ad:** black bar on ear-patch on white head; and **im:** like winter adult, but tail white with black tip; pinkish legs; white and black wing-tips, black trailing edge of wings, and blackish bar on upper wing-coverts. Flight resembles that of terns.

• Rare transient and winter visitor; lakes, large ponds.

Ring-billed Gull   *Larus delawarensis*

Id: 18"; **sum ad:** white head, tail, and underparts; black patch on yellow bill; black wing-tips with two white spots; legs yellow; eyes white; **win ad:** crown and hind-neck lightly mottled; **1st win:** profusely small-spotted or mottled head, breast, and wing-coverts; tail mottled grayish with broad black tail band; **2nd win:** somewhat more heavily mottled than winter adult, and has a rather narrow black tail band near tip.

• Transient and winter visitor; large ponds, lakes, landfills.

Herring Gull   *Larus argentatus*

Id: 24"; legs and feet pink at all ages; **sum ad:** small red bill-spot; little white in wing tip; eyes yellow; **win ad:** heavily mottled or streaked on head, neck, upper back and breast; darker and browner than other large gulls in our area; **1st win:** heavily streaked and mottled dark grayish brown; blackish tail; dark, barred upper tail-coverts; all-black bill; **2nd win:** paler and slightly grayer than first winter, with whitish upper tail-coverts and tail base; bill yellowish with black patch at tip.

• Rare transient and winter visitor; lakes, landfills.

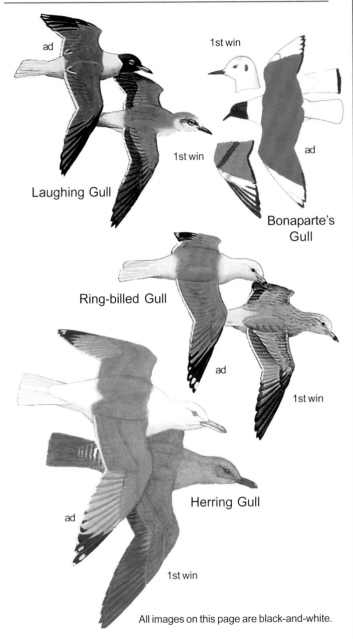

Laughing Gull

ad

1st win

1st win

Bonaparte's Gull

ad

Ring-billed Gull

ad

1st win

ad

Herring Gull

1st win

All images on this page are black-and-white.

37

Caspian Tern   *Sterna caspia*

Id: 22"; **sum ad:** has heavy red bill; tail moderately forked; wing-tips extend well beyond tail tip in perched bird; and **win ad + im:** forehead, fore-crown, eye-patch, as well as hind-crown and nape, mottled blackish.

• SD and BRP. Rare transient; lakes, reservoirs.

Common Tern   *Sterna hirundo*

Id: 15"; **sum ad:** mostly white, with pale gray back; upper surface of wings pale gray with a wedge-shaped blackish patch near wing-tip; forehead, crown and nape black; deeply forked tail; red legs; and red bill with (usually) black tip; **im + win ad:** bill all-black; black on head from eye to hind-crown to nape; blackish strip on upper side of leading edge of wing from wrist to shoulder.

• SD and VA BRP. Rare transient; lakes, ponds, and reservoirs.

Forster's Tern   *Sterna forsteri*

Id: 15"; like Common Tern, but tail grayish, more deeply forked; primaries whitish; *no* wedge-shaped patch near wing-tip; and **im + win ad:** *no* black bar on leading edge of wing from shoulder to wrist; black patch through eye, *not* on nape.

• SD and BRP. Rare transient; large ponds, lakes, reservoirs.

Black Tern   *Chlidonias niger*

Id: 10"; often seen in patchy molt; medium gray back and wings and (forked) tail; black bill; **sum ad:** black head and underparts, except white untacs; **win ad:** mostly white, with black hind-neck to ear-patch and eye; **im:** like winter adult, but back mottled brownish.

• SD and BRP. Rare transient; lakes, reservoirs, marshes, ponds.

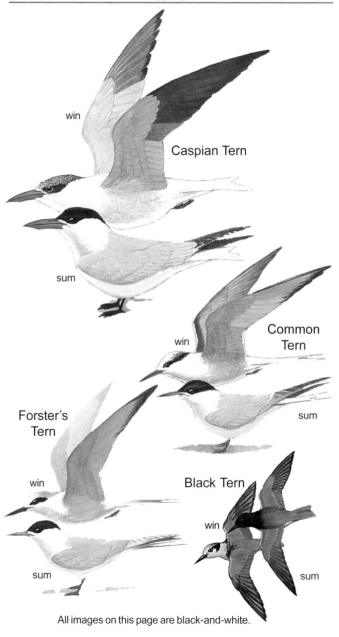

win

Caspian Tern

sum

win

Common
Tern

sum

Forster's
Tern

win

sum

Black Tern

win

sum

All images on this page are black-and-white.

39

Pheasants, Grouse, and Turkeys — Phasianidae

Ring-necked Pheasant   *Phasianus colchicus*

Id: m – 32", f – 21"; small head, heavy body, long pointed tail; **m:** head green and red; collar white; body and very long tail mostly iridescent bronzy, mottled and spotted; **f:** mostly buffy brown with mottling and spotting.

• SD and VA BRP. Rare year-round resident; meadows, partly overgrown fields, cropland, hedgerows.

Ruffed Grouse   *Bonasa umbellus*

Id: 17"; small head, heavy body, medium-long rounded tail; mottled upperparts, and broadly barred flanks and sides; plumage may be light gray or reddish brown, or an intermediate color; a blackish neck-ruff may show during the courtship drumming and display.

• Year-round resident; coniferous or deciduous forests, mixed, brushy second-growth and borders.

Wild Turkey   *Meleagris gallopavo*

Id: m – 45", f – 36"; small head, heavy body, medium-long rounded tail; plumage heavily barred blackish or dark brown, with iridescence.

• Year-round resident; coniferous, deciduous or mixed woods, secluded borders, clearings, meadows.

Quails — Odontophoridae

Northern Bobwhite   *Colinus virginianus*

Id: 9"; rather small head, heavy body, and short square tail; upperparts mottled blackish and brown; underparts mottled and barred and spotted blackish or brown on white; throat and superciliary line white (**m**) or buff (**f**). <u>V</u>: a loud whistle, *white* or *bob-white,* or *bob-bob-white*.

• Year-round resident; numbers variable, decreasing in recent years; open country with shrubs and grass, woodland borders, hedgerows, cultivated fields.

♀

♂
Ring-necked
Pheasant

Ruffed Grouse

Wild Turkey

♂
Northern
Bobwhite
♀

41

Vultures — Cathartidae

Black Vulture   *Coragyps atratus*

Id: 24"; like Turkey Vulture, with mostly black plumage, but tail short; wing-tips look broadly whitish from below; head black; legs medium gray. In flight it soars with wings straight out, and occasionally it flaps quickly several times, then glides.

• Year-round resident; flying over a wide variety of habitats.

Turkey Vulture   *Cathartes aura*

Id: 28"; plumage black except medium to dark gray flight feathers (as seen from below); tail rather long; **ad:** bare head, and legs, red; **im:** bare head blackish. In flight it soars with wings held slightly upward at an angle, and flaps very infrequently (and slowly).

• Year-round resident; flying over a wide variety of habitats.

Osprey, Eagles, and Hawks — Accipitridae

Osprey   *Pandion haliaetus*

Id: 23"; blackish above; white below; long wings angled at wrist (which has a blackish patch); head whitish, with broad black line through eye.

• Transient, and rare summer and very rare winter visitor; over rivers, lakes, ponds, marshes, tree-tops near water.

Bald Eagle   *Haliaeetus leucocephalus*

Id: 33"; **ad:** blackish brown except white head and white tail and large yellow bill; **im:** blackish brown; dull white tail base; dull whitish mottling under wings. See Golden Eagle — p. 48.

• Rare year-round resident; over woods or scattered trees along rivers, lake shores.

Black Vulture

Turkey Vulture

Osprey

im

Bald Eagle*

ad

ad

*black-and-white images

43

Northern Harrier   *Circus cyaneus*

Id: 19"; conspicuous white rump patch; long, barred tail; long wings; flaps and glides irregularly close to the ground; **m:** medium gray above; whitish below; and **f + im:** dark brown above; more cinnamon (and streaked) below.

• Transient and winter visitor; tall-grass fields, large marshes, open grassy plains.

Sharp-shinned Hawk   *Accipiter striatus*

Id: 12"; long, barred, *square*-tipped tail; rounded wings; **ad:** dark gray above; narrow reddish bars below; and **im:** dark grayish brown above; heavily streaked below. See Cooper's Hawk.

• Transient, winter visitor, and rare summer resident; forests, borders, broad hedgerows.

Cooper's Hawk   *Accipiter cooperii*

Id: 17"; like Sharp-shinned Hawk, but larger; tail *rounded* at tip.

• Year-round resident; dense to open woods, scattered trees, woodland borders.

Northern Goshawk   *Accipiter gentilis*

Id: 22"; long, barred tail; **ad:** medium bluish gray above; finely barred pale gray below; white line over eye; black patch behind eye; **im:** whitish line over eye; mottled dark brown above; whitish below, streaked and spotted blackish.

• Very rare transient and winter visitor; secluded high mountain forest, small openings, partial clearings.

ad ♀

ad ♂

im

Northern Harrier

ad

im

Sharp-shinned Hawk

ad

im

Cooper's Hawk

ad

im

Northern Goshawk

45

Red-shouldered Hawk
Buteo lineatus

Id: 20"; in flight, from below, shows a pale patch near wing-tip; **ad:** mottled dark and white above; narrow reddish bars below; chestnut "shoulder" patch; narrow white tail bars (2 or 3 visible) on dark gray; **im:** browner and more heavily streaked below than Broad-winged Hawk, and whitish tail bars are narrower, fainter, and more numerous; also there is usually a trace of adult's "shoulder" patch.

• Transient, and year-round resident; woods, forests, perched in open woodland borders; frequently near water.

Broad-winged Hawk
Buteo platypterus

Id: 17"; **ad:** dark grayish brown above, barred reddish below; broad white tail bars (1 or 2 visible) on blackish tail; **im:** streaked above and below; narrow tail bands. See Red-shouldered Hawk.

• Transient (flocks in the fall) and summer resident; nesting in extensive wooded areas, migrating over forests, woodlands, fields, ridge tops.

Red-tailed Hawk
Buteo jamaicensis

Id: 23"; **ad:** dark above; white below, with patchy belly-band; rufous tail; **im:** streaked below (less so on breast); narrow black tail bars on gray.

• Year-round resident; over grassy plains, forests, woodlands, open brushy country, borders.

Rough-legged Hawk
Buteo lagopus

Id: 22"; broad dark sub-terminal tail band; basally the tail is mostly white (**f,**) or barred gray and white (**m**); flight feathers mostly white with black tips, as seen from below; tarsi feathered; **light morph:** heavily streaked head, back, and breast; black belly and flanks; **dark morph**: head, back, underparts, and under wing-coverts blackish brown.

• SD and BRP. Rare transient and winter visitor; open areas, partly overgrown fields.

Red-shouldered Hawk

ad

Broad-winged Hawk

im

ad

im

Red-tailed Hawk

ad

im

Rough-legged Hawk

light morph
ad ♀

dark morph
ad ♂

Golden Eagle   *Aquila chrysaetos*

Id: 34"; wings long, tail rather short; tarsi feathered; **ad:** dark brown with tawny crown and nape; faint grayish tail bars; **im:** rather contrasty white patch at base of inner primaries below; tail white basally, broadly black-tipped.

• Rare transient and winter visitor, and very rare in summer; dry mountain slopes, open woods and brushland, cliffs.

Falcons — Falconidae

American Kestrel   *Falco sparverius*

Id: 11"; rump and back, reddish brown, barred with black; two broad black lines down side of face; underparts whitish or buffy; **m:** spotted below; wings bluish spotted with black; tail plain rufous with black bar near tip; **f:** streaked below; wings and tail rufous spotted with black.

• Year-round resident, rare in summer; dry open areas, tree-dotted fields, forest borders, utility poles or wires.

Merlin   *Falco columbarius*

Id: 12"; streaked below; **m:** bluish gray above; tail barred black and gray. **f + im:** brown above; tail dark brown and gray. See American Kestrel.

• Rare transient and winter visitor; large open areas, scattered trees, woodland borders.

Peregrine Falcon   *Falco peregrinus*

Id: 19"; dark bluish gray above; black crown with broad black stripe down side of face; spotted and barred below, except whitish throat and breast; tail barred; **im:** like adult, but dark brown; heavily streaked below.

• Rare year-round resident; secluded cliffs or ledges, rocky canyons, open mountain-tops and high ridges.

im
(x 0.5)

Golden Eagle

ad

♀

♂

American
Kestrel

ad ♂

♀ + im

Merlin

Peregrine Falcon

Pigeons and Doves — Columbidae

Rock Pigeon   *Columba livia*

Id: 13"; variable; white to nearly black, variegated or uniform; many individuals are close to the original wild type from Europe, which is mostly medium bluish gray, with iridescent green and purple collar; two broad black wing bars; white rump; broad black tail tip band; legs red.

• Year-round resident; cities, towns, farms, near horse stables or barns.

Mourning Dove   *Zenaida macroura*

Id: 12"; brownish gray above, with darker wings; grayish buff below; medium-long, narrow, wedge-shaped tail; tail feathers mostly gray with white-tips.

• Year-round resident; hedgerows, woods, croplands, borders, suburban areas.

Cuckoos — Cuculidae

Black-billed Cuckoo   *Coccyzus erythropthalmus*

Id: 12"; like Yellow-billed Cuckoo, but bill black; eye-ring red; *no* rufous on wing; white tips on tail feathers very narrow; form narrow bars across tail.

• Rare transient and summer resident; second-growth, borders, deciduous forest.

Yellow-billed Cuckoo   *Coccyzus americanus*

Id: 12"; brown above; white below; bill black above, buffy yellow below, slightly decurved; inner webs of primaries rufous, forming a wing-patch in flight; tail graduated, black with long white feather-tip spots.

• Transient and summer resident; deciduous forest, second-growth, borders.

Rock Pigeon

Mourning Dove

wing of Yellow-billed Cuckoo

Black-billed Cuckoo

Yellow-billed Cuckoo

Barn Owls — Tytonidae

Barn Owl *Tyto alba*

Id: 15"; buffy brown above, mottled and barred; white or buff below, with scattered small spots; face heart-shaped, white or buff. V̲: a single raspy, hiss-like screech.

• Rare year-round resident; old buildings, barns, or hunting at night in fields and woodland borders.

Typical Owls — Strigidae

Eastern Screech-Owl *Megascops asio*

Id: 8"; **gray morph:** pale to medium gray all over; streaked, mottled, barred and spotted; facial disk has black border and white "V" above bill, leading to prominent "ear"-tufts; eyes bright yellow; **red morph:** like gray morph, but rufous replaces most of gray; *not* as heavily streaked. V̲: a mellow or wailing tremolo, either descending or on one pitch.

• Year-round resident; woods, river borders, second-growth.

Great Horned Owl *Bubo virginianus*

Id: 21"; mostly brownish buff below, finely barred dark brown; throat and center of chest white; upperparts streaked, mottled, and barred blackish brown; face rufous with black border; medium-length "ear"-tufts; eyes yellow. V̲: a low-pitched, rather musical *hoo, hoo-hoo-hoo, hoo.*

• Year-round resident; old-growth forests, woodlots, borders.

Barred Owl *Strix varia*

Id: 20"; brownish gray; underparts mostly heavily streaked, but barred on throat and upper chest; barred on head and upperparts; *no* "ear"-tufts; eyes brown. V̲: a loud ascending *ho-hoo ho-hoo, ho-hoo ho-hoo-ah.*

• Year-round resident; old coniferous and deciduous forests, moist woods.

Barn Owl

Eastern
Screech-Owl
(gray and red
morphs)

Barred Owl

Great Horned Owl

Long-eared Owl   *Asio otus*

Id: 15"; like a small, slender Great Horned Owl, but ear tufts longer and attached closer to the center of its face. <u>V</u>: a slow series of hoots on one pitch.

• Rare and irregular year-round resident, more often seen in winter; coniferous forests.

Short-eared Owl   *Asio flammeus*

Id: 16"; streaked tawny and brown above and below; but whitish belly and under tail-coverts; sooty around eyes; white between eyes; and "ear" tufts very short, close together. Often hunts in daylight, flight buoyant and somewhat erratic.

• Rare transient and winter visitor; grassy open country.

Northern Saw-whet Owl   *Aegolius acadicus*

Id: 7"; **ad:** dark brown above, with white spots; whitish below, with rufous streaks; head appears square; **im:** head and breast chocolate brown; belly tawny rufous; white between eyes. <u>V</u>: a series of evenly spaced mellow single notes.

• Rarely seen or heard transient and winter visitor (but now known to be fairly common in fall migration) in wooded or brushy areas; also year-round resident above 4000 feet elevation in coniferous forest, or dense mixed or deciduous forest.

Nightjars — Caprimulgidae

Common Nighthawk   *Chordeiles minor*

Id: 9"; mostly shades of gray; long slender wings with broad white bar across primaries (shows in flight); throat white or grayish buff; underparts narrowly barred; *no* white tail tips. <u>V</u>: a nasal, rasping *peent*.

• Transient; also summer resident near SD and VA BRP, but declining in numbers; over open areas, fields, cities, towns; often seen in loose flocks during migration.

Long-eared
Owl

Short-eared Owl

ad

Northern
Saw-whet Owl

im

Common Nighthawk

55

Chuck-will's-widow   *Caprimulgus carolinensis*

Id: 11"; mottled dark buffy reddish brown; white throat-bar; **m:** two large tail patches white above, buffy below; **f:** *no* tail patches. <u>V</u>: a loud whistle, *chuck-will's-widow.*
 • Rare transient and summer resident; thickets, undergrowth, woodland borders.

Whip-poor-will   *Caprimulgus vociferus*

Id: 10"; mottled grayish brown above; barred brownish gray below; **m:** throat-bar and very large space on tail corners white; **f:** throat bar and very small tail patches pale dull buffy. <u>V</u>: *whip-poor-will.*
 • Transient and summer resident; woodland borders, clearings, second-growth.

Swifts — Apodidae

Chimney Swift   *Chaetura pelagica*

Id: 5.3"; blackish brown; throat pale gray; tail short, square; wings narrow, pointed. <u>V</u>: high-pitched, rapid, chipping notes.
 • Transient and summer resident; over open country, mixed woods and fields; nests and roosts mainly in chimneys.

Hummingbirds — Trochilidae

Ruby-throated Hummingbird   *Archilochus colubris*

Id: 3.7"; greenish above; tail feathers pointed; **m:** tail forked, throat iridescent red, breast and belly mostly whitish; **f:** black tail white-tipped, not forked; underparts whitish.
 • Transient and summer resident; mixed woods and fields, borders, gardens, parks; readily visits sugar-water feeders.

Chuck-will's-widow*

Whip-poor-will*

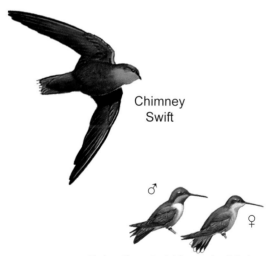

Chimney
Swift

Ruby-throated Hummingbird

*black-and-white images

Kingfishers — Alcedinidae

Belted Kingfisher   *Ceryle alcyon*

Id: 13"; grayish blue above; **m:** white below with blue chest-band; **f:** three broad bands below: blue upper, white middle, rufous lower; belly and under tail-coverts white.

• Year-round resident; dives into rivers, lakes, ponds for food; nests in nearby dirt banks.

Woodpeckers — Picidae

Red-headed Woodpecker   *Melanerpes erythrocephalus*

Id: 9.5"; **ad:** head entirely red; upperparts blackish blue, with broadly white rump patch and wing patches; breast and belly white; **im:** head dark brown; upperparts mostly blackish brown with white rump, and some white on wing; underparts white with dark brown streaks on throat and breast.

• Rare year-round resident; forests, scattered woodlots, especially White Oak woods in years when acorns are abundant.

Red-bellied Woodpecker   *Melanerpes carolinus*

Id: 9.5"; back narrowly barred black and white; rump-patch white; underparts mostly pale gray with inconspicuous pink wash on belly; **m:** forehead, crown, and nape bright red; **f:** red restricted to nasal tufts and nape.

• Year-round resident; open or dense woods, borders, suburban residential areas, parks.

Yellow-bellied Sapsucker   *Sphyrapicus varius*

Id: 8.5"; **m:** crown and throat red; black throat-border and chest-band; black above, barred with whitish; long white patch on wing; rump-patch white; **f:** like male, but chin and upper throat white; **im + part of 1st win**: mostly barred blackish and brown above and below; long white patch on wing; gradually acquires adult plumage through winter and early spring.

• Transient and winter resident (and rare year-round resident on higher slopes and ridge-tops); open woods, hardwood forests, borders, second-growth.

Belted Kingfisher

♀

♂

Red-headed Woodpecker

ad

im

im

ad ♂

ad ♀

Red-bellied Woodpecker

♂

♀

Yellow-bellied Sapsucker

Downy Woodpecker — *Picoides pubescens*

Id: 7"; like Hairy Woodpecker but smaller, and much smaller-billed; usually has blackish spots on white outer tail feathers.
• Year-round resident; forests, woodlands, suburban areas.

Hairy Woodpecker — *Picoides villosus*

Id: 9"; underparts, back-stripe, wing-spots, part of cheek, line over eye, and outer-tail feathers white; wings, scapulars, some head markings, and central tail feathers black; **m:** small red nape-patch; **f:** *no* red.
• Year-round resident; mountain forests, open woods, borders.

Northern Flicker — *Colaptes auratus*

Id: ("Yellow-shafted" Flicker) **12"**; brown above, barred black, with white rump; grayish crown and nape, with red nape-patch; throat and face buffy gray; black chest-band; black-spotted whitish breast and belly; yellow under-wings and tail base; **m:** has black mustache mark; **f:** *no* mustache mark.
• Transient and year-round resident; oak woods, borders, partial clearings, suburban areas, campgrounds.

Pileated Woodpecker — *Dryocopus pileatus*

Id: 16"; black, with white lines on face and neck; prominent crest bright red; iris yellow; under wing-coverts white; **m:** base of bill to tip of crest red, and malar streak mostly red; **f:** forehead and malar streak black.
• Year-round resident; deciduous forest, patchy old woods, wooded parks and borders near extensive woodlands.

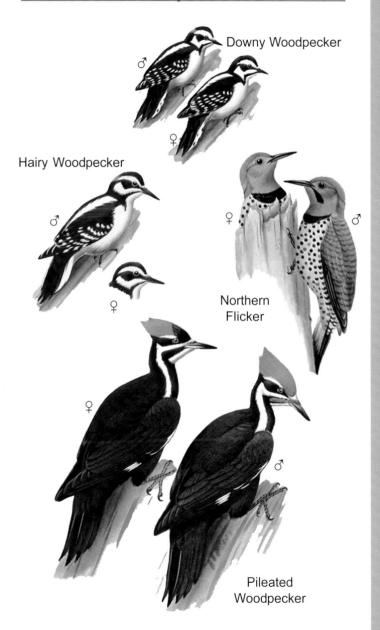

Downy Woodpecker

♂

♀

Hairy Woodpecker

♂

♀

♀

Northern
Flicker

♂

♀

♂

Pileated
Woodpecker

Flycatchers — Tyrannidae

Olive-sided Flycatcher   *Contopus cooperi*

   Id: 7.5"; grayish olive above, and on sides and flanks; throat and center of breast and belly white; partly hidden white patch on each side of rump.

   • Rare transient (and formerly very rare and erratic summer resident at high elevations); dead, open, upper branches and tree-tops in coniferous forests, borders, partial clearings.

Eastern Wood-Pewee   *Contopus virens*

   Id: 6"; whitish to pale gray below, dark gray above; lower mandible pale yellowish. <u>V</u>: a plaintive *pee-a-wee*, or *pe-wee*.

   • Transient and summer resident; river-border woods, forest borders, mixed conifers and hardwoods.

Yellow-bellied Flycatcher   *Empidonax flaviventris*

   Id: 5.5"; like Acadian Flycatcher, but yellower below, and darker above, and wing shows only a moderate extension of primary feathers beyond secondaries in folded wing-tip (mpx). <u>V</u>: a quiet, rising *cur-lee*.

   • Rare transient (and formerly very rare summer resident at high elevations); thickets, woodlands, old-growth forests.

Acadian Flycatcher   *Empidonax virescens*

   Id: 5.7"; mostly olive above, but wings blackish brown with whitish bars; pale yellowish to whitish eye-ring; throat and lower breast whitish; chest and sides grayish olive; belly pale yellow to whitish; bill nearly as broad (at base) as long, and yellowish below; wing shows a long extension of primary feathers beyond secondaries in folded wing-tip (lpx). <u>V</u>: a loud, abrupt *pit-seek*; also a quiet chatter.

   • Transient and summer resident; wooded stream valleys and moist ravines.

Olive-sided Flycatcher

Eastern Wood-Pewee

Yellow-bellied Flycatcher

Acadian Flycatcher

Alder Flycatcher   *Empidonax alnorum*

Id: 5.7"; like Acadian Flycatcher, but darker and browner above and on chest; eye-ring less distinct; bill more orange below; wing shows a moderate extension of primary feathers beyond secondaries in folded wing-tip (mpx). <u>V</u>: *fee-bee-o.*

• Transient, and rare summer resident; borders, hedgerows; shrubby young second-growth, ridge-top thickets.

Willow Flycatcher   *Empidonax traillii*

Id: 5.7"; like Alder Flycatcher, wing shows a moderate extension of primary feathers beyond secondaries in folded wing-tip (mpx), but the plumage is slightly browner above; and the eye-ring is even less prominent. <u>V</u>: an abrupt *fitz-bew.*

• Transient and rare summer resident; moist thickets, partial clearings, borders; in summer in wet meadows or undergrowth along streams.

Least Flycatcher   *Empidonax minimus*

Id: 5.3"; like Acadian Flycatcher, but smaller; head and upperparts darker; belly slightly yellower; throat slightly whiter; bill paler below, with dark tip; wing shows a short extension of primary feathers beyond secondaries in folded wing-tip (spx). <u>V</u>: an abrupt, unmusical, oft-repeated *chi-bec.*

• Rare and scattered transient and summer resident; open woods, thickets, borders, wooded parks, large suburban gardens.

Eastern Phoebe   *Sayornis phoebe*

Id: 7"; like Eastern Wood-Pewee, but yellower below; head darker; *no* wing-bars; bill black; usually pumps tail after landing on a perch. <u>V</u>: a somewhat rasping *fee-bee.*

• Year-round resident, but rare and at lower elevations in winter; usually near streams or rivers, nesting under bridges, in crevices in cliffs, in eaves of houses or cabins.

Great Crested Flycatcher   *Myiarchus crinitus*

Id: 8.7"; upperparts grayish olive; throat, chest and head medium gray, contrasting with yellow belly; bill orange at base below. <u>V</u>: a loud, drawn-out, rolling *reeeep.*

• Transient and summer resident; borders, open woods, partial clearings; often seen in the tops of dead or partly dead trees, where it nests in tree-holes.

Willow Flycatcher

Alder Flycatcher

Least Flycatcher

Eastern
Phoebe

Great
Crested
Flycatcher

Eastern Kingbird   *Tyrannus tyrannus*

Id: 8.5"; upperparts blackish to dark gray; underparts and tail-tip band white.

• Transient and summer resident; pastures, hay fields, borders, hedgerows, clearings.

Shrikes — Laniidae

Loggerhead Shrike   *Lanius ludovicianus*

Id: 9"; gray and white with black mask; the wings and tail show white patches; bill short, stout, hooked at tip, black.

• Rare (and numbers dwindling) year-round resident; open dry overgrown fields, hedgerows, brushy areas, borders; mostly at lower elevations.

Vireos — Vireonidae

White-eyed Vireo   *Vireo griseus*

Id: 4.5"; grayish green above; pale yellowish wing-bars; yellow eye-ring and lores; whitish below with yellow wash; eyes white. <u>V</u>: a staccato *chík-per-whéeoo-chík*.

• Transient and summer resident; usually near water, in thickets, hedgerows, borders, brushy stream valleys.

Yellow-throated Vireo   *Vireo flavifrons*

Id: 5.5"; yellow-green above; two white wing-bars; yellow "spectacles;" yellow throat and breast; white belly.

• Transient and summer resident; open woods, wooded river valleys, borders, partial clearings.

Blue-headed Vireo   *Vireo solitarius*

Id: 5"; gray above; bluish gray head; prominent white "spectacles;" white wing-bars on blackish wings; white below, with yellowish sides and flanks.

• Year-round resident, but very rare in winter; dry, brushy woods, deciduous forest, mixed conifers and hardwoods.

Eastern
Kingbird

Loggerhead
Shrike

White-eyed Vireo

Yellow-throated Vireo

Blue-headed Vireo

Warbling Vireo   *Vireo gilvus*

Id: 5.5"; gray or olive-gray above, including crown; whitish below, with sides tinged greenish olive; gray line through eye; white line over eye; *no* wing-bars.
• Rare summer resident and transient; mostly in tree-tops along river banks, also city parks, suburban areas.

Philadelphia Vireo   *Vireo philadelphicus*

Id: 5"; small-billed like Warbling Vireo, but grayer above; has darker line through eye; and more yellowish breast.
• Rare transient; open woods, borders, partial clearings.

Red-eyed Vireo   *Vireo olivaceus*

Id: 6"; olive-green above, white below; crown medium-gray, narrowly black-bordered; white line over eye; dark line through eye; eyes red (**ad**) or brownish (**im**).
• Transient and summer resident; dense or open forest, wooded riversides, wooded parks, forest borders.

Jays, Crows, and Ravens — Corvidae

Blue Jay   *Cyanocitta cristata*

Id: 11"; crested; upperparts medium grayish blue, with black bars on wings and tail, and white spots and a white bar on the wings; pale gray below, with a black "necklace."
• Transient and year-round resident; coniferous and deciduous forest, second-growth, borders, parks, campgrounds.

American Crow   *Corvus brachyrhynchos*

Id: 17"; black all over; tail square-tipped; larger than Fish Crow, smaller than Raven. <u>V</u>: a harsh *kaah*.
• Year-round resident; grassy fields, mixed woods and farm land, woodland borders, hedgerows; often in large flocks.

Warbling Vireo

Philadelphia
Vireo

Red-eyed Vireo

Blue Jay

American Crow

69

Fish Crow   *Corvus ossifragus*

   Id: 15"; like American Crow, but smaller, and voice different — a more abrupt *kahk*, or *kahk-kahk*.

   • SD and VA BRP. Irregular year-round resident; occurs especially near lowland rivers, also around farms and suburban areas.

Common Raven   *Corvus corax*

   Id: 25"; black all over; throat shaggy; head and bill relatively large; tail wedge-shaped. <u>V</u>: a croaking sound, lower-pitched than that of the American Crow or Fish Crow.

   • Year-round resident; spruce-fir or hardwood forests on rocky mountain-sides and ridge-tops, cliffs, campgrounds, occasionally over lower slopes and nearby flatlands.

Larks — Alaudidae

Horned Lark   *Eremophila alpestris*

   Id: 7"; **m:** streaked brownish above; mostly white below, with black breast-band and black on face; short black feather "horns" at rear corners of crown; tail black below, with white margins; **f + win m:** duller; **im:** faint face-pattern and breast-band; tail as in adult; *no* "horns."

   • Transient and localized year-round resident; short-grass fields, open ridge tops and slopes, farm fields.

Swallows — Hirundinidae

Purple Martin   *Progne subis*

   Id: 8"; **m:** black with purplish gloss; **f + im:** dark bluish brown above, slightly glossy; pale gray to grayish brown below, with obscure darker "scales" and spots.

   • Transient, and scattered summer resident in lowlands where multi-unit nesting boxes or groups of gourds are provided; over open country, farms, suburban areas, along woodland borders.

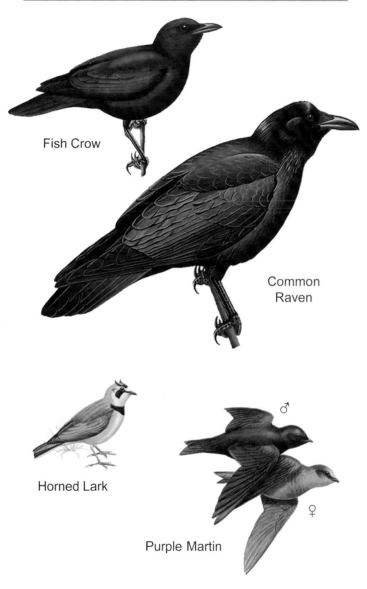

Fish Crow

Common
Raven

Horned Lark

♂

♀

Purple Martin

71

Tree Swallow   *Tachycineta bicolor*

Id: 5.5"; **ad:** most are glossy dark greenish blue above, but some females are much browner; white below; **im:** dark brown above; white below; very pale breast-band.

• Transient and summer resident, nesting near SD and VA BRP, and increasingly farther south; farmlands, grassy open areas, clearings; often near ponds, lakes, rivers.

Northern Rough-winged Swallow
Stelgidopteryx serripennis

Id: 5"; dark grayish brown above; whitish below with brownish wash on throat; tail short. See Bank Swallow.

• Transient and summer resident; near road cuts, river banks; nests singly in dirt banks.

Bank Swallow   *Riparia riparia*

Id: 5"; much like Rough-winged Swallow, but throat white; dark band across breast.

• Transient throughout the area, and rare summer resident near SD and VA BRP; often in flocks over pastures, lakes, rivers; nests in colonies in dirt or gravel banks.

Cliff Swallow   *Petrochelidon pyrrhonota*

Id: 5.5"; **ad:** forehead very pale buff; much of throat and face rufous; lower throat blackish; rump buffy; back blackish, with whitish streaks; **im:** mostly darker and duller, especially on head.

• Transient and localized summer resident; near bridges, dams, lakes, farm buildings; nests in colonies.

Barn Swallow   *Hirundo rustica*

Id: 6"; glossy blackish blue above; mostly rufous below, with incomplete blackish breast-band; tail long, very deeply forked; **im:** duller; tail shorter.

• Transient and summer resident; parks, fields, farmlands, near bridges or old buildings.

Northern
Rough-winged
Swallow

ad ♂

Tree
Swallow

im

Bank Swallow

Cliff
Swallow

Barn
Swallow

Chickadees and Titmice — Paridae

Carolina Chickadee   *Poecile carolinensis*

Id: 4.5"; mostly medium to pale gray above and whitish below; with black throat and top of head. <u>V</u>: a high-pitched *four*-noted song, *dee-dee, dee-dee.*

• Year-round resident, rare above 4000 feet elevation; forests, parks, suburban areas, farm woodlots, hedgerows.

Black-capped Chickadee   *Poecile atricapillus*

Id: 5"; like Carolina Chickadee, but black throat-patch slightly larger, and lower border of patch not as sharply defined; whitish edges of secondary wing-feathers contrast more noticeably with basic gray of the wings. <u>V</u>: a high-pitched *two*-noted song, *dee-dee.*

• Year-round resident; mainly in GSM and near the southern end of NC BRP in coniferous or deciduous forests, or forest borders, above 4000 feet elevation in summer; ranges much lower in winter. Hybridizes with Carolina Chickadee at many locations where their summer ranges meet.

Tufted Titmouse   *Baeolophus bicolor*

Id: 6.5"; crested; pale to medium gray above; whitish below, with pale rufous flanks.

• Year-round resident, rare at highest elevations; forests, second-growth woods, parks, suburban areas, campgrounds.

Carolina
Chickadee

Black-capped
Chickadee

Tufted
Titmouse

Nuthatches — Sittidae

Red-breasted Nuthatch *Sitta canadensis*

Id: 4"; **ad:** like White-breasted Nuthatch, but smaller; rufous below; long black line through eye (and white line over eye); **f + im:** paler and duller. May move head-first down tree trunks.

• Year-round resident in forests at high elevations, mainly very irregular (in numbers) transient and winter visitor at lower elevations; pine woods , other coniferous forest.

White-breasted Nuthatch *Sitta carolinensis*

Id: 5.5"; **m:** gray above; crown and hind-neck black; white below; some rufous on thighs, belly, or under tail-coverts; white patches on black tail; **f:** duller; crown gray. May move head-first down tree trunks.

• Year-round resident; deciduous forest, borders, woodlots, suburban areas.

Brown-headed Nuthatch *Sitta pusilla*

Id: 4.5"; medium to dark gray above, with brown crown, and black line through eye; whitish below with a tinge of buff.

• BRP. Rare and localized year-round resident; pine woods at low elevations. May move head-first down tree trunks.

Creepers — Certhiidae

Brown Creeper *Certhia americana*

Id: 5"; streaked dark brown and pale brown above; plain white to pale buff below; tail long and slender; spread wings show a pale buff band; creeps *up* (but *not* down) tree trunks and large branches.

• Transient and winter visitor at lower elevations; rare year-round resident above 4000 feet elevation; coniferous forest at high elevations in summer, various wooded habitats in fall, winter, and spring.

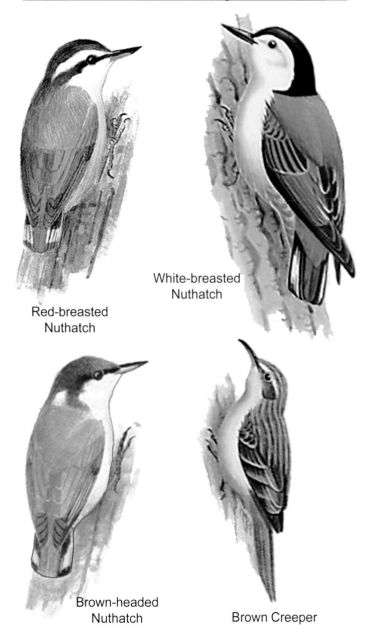

Red-breasted
Nuthatch

White-breasted
Nuthatch

Brown-headed
Nuthatch

Brown Creeper

Wrens — Troglodytidae

Carolina Wren   *Thryothorus ludovicianus*
    Id: 5.5"; rufous brown upperparts; conspicuous white line over eye; rich tawny-rufous on breast; barred wings and tail; and barred under tail-coverts. <u>V</u>: a rollicking *toreetle-toreetle-toreetle* — may be heard almost any month of the year.
    • Year-round resident; backyards, gardens, woods, borders, deciduous forest undergrowth.

House Wren   *Troglodytes aedon*
    Id: 5"; dull reddish-brown above; pale dull grayish brown below; wings, tail, flanks, and under tail-coverts barred; tail short; faint buffy line over eye; **im:** "scaly" lower throat and breast. <u>V</u>: an extended, bubbly, warbling.
    • Transient, summer resident, and rare winter visitor; hedgerows, borders, overgrown fields, suburbs.

Winter Wren   *Troglodytes troglodytes*
    Id: 4"; dark brown above; paler brown below; heavily barred belly, flanks, and under tail-coverts; very short tail; short bill. <u>V</u>: very complex, lengthy, and musical song.
    • Year-round resident above 3500 feet elevation; transient and winter resident throughout; brushy ravines, forest undergrowth, dense borders, wooded streams.

Sedge Wren   *Cistothorus platensis*
    Id: 4.5"; back streaked black and whitish; crown finely streaked blackish brown and buff; underparts whitish, tinged pale rufous; under tail-coverts *not* barred; tail and bill short.
    • Rare transient; open grassy or sedgy marshes, wet meadows, dense tall grass.

Marsh Wren   *Cistothorus palustris*
    Id: 5"; like Sedge Wren, but crown blackish and reddish brown, and *not* streaked; back streaks more contrasty; white line over eye much more prominent, and bill and tail longer. <u>V</u>: a metallic, rattling song; and a metallic *chuck*.
    • Rare transient; marshes, marshy borders of ponds, streams, lakes.

Carolina Wren

House Wren

Winter Wren

Sedge Wren

Marsh Wren

Kinglets — Regulidae

Golden-crowned Kinglet *Regulus satrapa*

Id: 3.7"; **m:** grayish olive above, paler below; two white wing-bars; head striped black and white; with orange crown patch, tiny bill; **f:** crown-patch yellow.

• Year-round resident in high-elevation forests of conifers; transient and winter resident in woodland borders, second-growth, pine woods.

Ruby-crowned Kinglet *Regulus calendula*

Id: 3.7"; resembles Golden-crowned Kinglet, but head and face mostly greenish gray, and *not* striped; has white eye-ring; flicks wings as it hops among the twigs and branches; **m:** has red crown-patch (usually hidden).

• Transient and winter resident; forest, open woods, thickets, borders.

Gnatcatchers — Sylviidae

Blue-gray Gnatcatcher *Polioptila caerulea*

Id: 4.5"; **m:** pale bluish gray above; white below; white feather-edgings on blackish wings; forehead and sides of crown narrowly black; eye-ring white; long tail mostly black above, white below; **f:** paler, duller, *no* black on head.

• Transient and summer resident; thickets, open woods, borders, second-growth, stream valleys.

Bluebirds, Thrushes, and Robins — Turdidae

Eastern Bluebird *Sialia sialis*

Id: 6.5"; **m:** uniform medium blue above; throat and breast bright rufous; belly and under tail-coverts white; **f:** paler, duller; in worn plumage may appear very drab; **im:** heavily spotted above and below.

• Year-round resident; old orchards, borders, partial clearings, hedgerows, farmland.

Golden-crowned
Kinglet

♂

♀

Ruby-crowned
Kinglet

♀

♂

Blue-gray
Gnatcatcher

♂

♀

Eastern Bluebird

im

Veery   *Catharus fuscescens*

Id: 7"; tawny-brown above; whitish or buffy below; breast *lightly* spotted dark brown.

• Transient and summer resident on middle to upper mountain slopes; deciduous forest, mixed woods, borders.

Gray-cheeked Thrush   *Catharus minimus*

Id: 7"; like Swainson's Thrush, but has grayish cheeks, and less noticeable eye-ring.

• Rare transient; borders, forest floor, old second-growth, mature forest.

Swainson's Thrush   *Catharus ustulatus*

Id: 7"; olive-brown above; prominent buffy eye-ring, and brownish-buff cheeks; mainly whitish below, but heavily dark-spotted on buffy breast.

• Transient; in dense forest, old second-growth, along forest borders; also rare summer resident in coniferous forest atop Mount Rogers, just outside of our area near VA BRP.

Hermit Thrush   *Catharus guttatus*

Id: 6.5"; like Swainson's Thrush, but has browner cheeks and back, *no* conspicuous eye-ring, and contrasty reddish brown rump, upper tail-coverts, and tail.

• Transient and winter resident; gardens, borders, dense forest, partial clearings; also summer resident in coniferous forest (above 5000 feet elevation).

Wood Thrush   *Hylocichla mustelina*

Id: 7.5"; more boldly spotted, and heavier-bodied, than other similar thrushes; contrasty bright rufous on head and upper back.

• Transient and summer resident; mature forest, old second-growth, borders, shrub-gardens bordering forest, suburban areas.

Veery

Gray-cheeked Thrush

Swainson's Thrush

Hermit Thrush

Wood Thrush

American Robin   *Turdus migratorius*

Id: 10"; **m**; blackish and dark gray above; eye-ring white; breast broadly brownish orange; throat white, streaked black; **f:** slightly paler and duller; **im:** heavily spotted below.

• Transient, summer resident, and winter visitor; gardens, hedgerows, borders, forest, second-growth.

Thrashers — Mimidae

Gray Catbird   *Dumetella carolinensis*

Id: 8"; slate gray, with black cap and dark reddish brown under tail-coverts.

• Transient and summer resident (numbers decreasing in recent years); undergrowth, partial clearings, borders, hedgerows, gardens.

Northern Mockingbird   *Mimus polyglottos*

Id: 10"; pale to medium gray above; whitish below; wing-bars and sides of tail white; large white wing-patch shows in flight; iris pale yellow to whitish; **im:** spotty streaks below.

• Year-round resident; thickets, hedgerows, farms, gardens, parks, borders.

Brown Thrasher   *Toxostoma rufum*

Id: 11"; upperparts and head reddish brown; underparts pale buff to whitish with heavy blackish-brown spotty streaks; iris yellow.

• Transient, summer resident, and frequent winter visitor; hedgerows, borders, scrubby woods, thickets, gardens.

im

ad

American Robin

Gray Catbird

Northern Mockingbird

Brown Thrasher

Starlings — Sturnidae

European Starling   *Sturnus vulgaris*

   Id: 8"; basically black; tail short; bill straight, rather slender, and pointed; **win:** has many small buff spots, which wear away gradually; bill black; **sum:** obscurely speckled; bill yellow; **im:** dark brownish gray all over.

   • Year-round resident, mostly in the lowlands; parks, pastures, farms, woodlots; often in large flocks; nests in crevices in brick or stone buildings, or in new or used woodpecker-holes or other cavities.

Pipits — Motacillidae

American Pipit   *Anthus rubescens*

   Id: 6"; grayish-olive above; buffy to whitish below, with white outer tail feathers, and blackish legs; dark streaks most prominent in fall and winter. Bobs tail as it walks.

   • Rare transient and winter visitor; short grass or bare open fields, lake shores, pastures.

Waxwings — Bombycillidae

Cedar Waxwing   *Bombycilla cedrorum*

   Id: 6"; crested; **ad:** has sleek brown plumage; paler below, with a faint yellowish tinge; chin, upper throat and mask black; yellow-tipped gray and black tail; may have waxy red tips on secondary wing-feathers; **im:** paler and duller; streaked above and below.

   • Irregular year-round resident; often in flocks in gardens, parks, open woods, borders, orchards.

sum

win

European Starling

im

sum

American Pipit

win

ad

Cedar Waxwing

im

Wood Warblers — Parulidae

Blue-winged Warbler   *Vermivora pinus*

Id: 4.5"; **m:** hind-neck and upperparts olive; head and under-parts mostly bright yellow; black line through eye; white bars on bluish wings; **f:** similar pattern but paler and duller.

• Rare transient and summer resident; brushy second-growth, thickets, borders.

Golden-winged Warbler   *Vermivora chrysoptera*

Id: 4.5"; **m:** bluish gray above, with yellow crown; black ear-patch and throat; yellow marks on wing; **f:** similar pattern but paler and duller.

• Rare transient and summer resident; brushy second-growth, borders, overgrown clearings.

Golden-winged Warbler x Blue-winged Warbler hybrids

"Brewster's" Warbler: like Blue-winged, but white mostly replaces yellow. **"Lawrence's" Warbler:** like Golden-winged, but yellow mostly replaces white.

Tennessee Warbler   *Vermivora peregrina*

Id: 4.5" sum m: grayish green above, white below; head pale gray; white throat and line over eye; **f + win m + im:** more yellowish overall; faint wing-bar.

• Transient, more often seen in the fall; open woods, borders, hedgerows.

Orange-crowned Warbler   *Vermivora celata*

Id: 4.5"; greenish gray above; yellowish gray below, with faint dark streaks; faint line over eye; hidden crown-patch.

• Rare transient; open woods, thickets, parks, borders.

Blue-winged
Warbler

Golden-winged
Warbler

♂

♀

"Brewster's"
Warbler

"Lawrence's"
Warbler

Blue-winged x Golden-winged hybrids

♂

♀

Tennessee
Warbler

Orange-crowned Warbler

89

Nashville Warbler *Vermivora ruficapilla*

Id: 4.5"; greenish olive above; wings darker; white eye-ring; gray head with reddish brown crown-patch; bright yellow below, except white patch on belly; **f + im:** similar but slightly duller.
• Transient, more numerous in the fall; open or dense woods, thickets, parks, borders.

Northern Parula *Parula americana*

Id: 4.5"; **m:** grayish blue above; yellowish olive back-patch; yellow throat and breast, black and reddish patch on lower throat and chest; belly, partial eye-ring, and wing-bars, white; **f:** paler and greener above; only a trace of breast-patch, or none.
• Transient and summer resident; wooded riversides, hardwood or mixed forest, borders.

Yellow Warbler *Dendroica petechia*

Id: 4.5"; **m:** greenish yellow above; rufous streaks on bright yellow below; tail yellow below; **f:** unstreaked, yellowish.
• Transient and summer resident; parks, scrubby woods, wooded riversides, scattered trees, borders.

Chestnut-sided Warbler *Dendroica pensylvanica*

Id: 4.5"; **sum ad:** back heavily streaked, black on yellowish green; two white wing-bars; white below with broad chestnut streak on side; black line through eye; **im + win ad:** bright yellow-green above; white below; and has wing-bars; *no* black on face; may show trace of rufous on sides.
• Transient and summer resident; open forest, brushy second-growth, open scrubby woods, borders.

Magnolia Warbler *Dendroica magnolia*

Id: 4.5"; **sum m:** much like Yellow-rumped Warbler, blackish above; heavily streaked below, but on yellow, *not* white; tail viewed from below is mostly white with a broad black tail-tip band; **f:** duller; mostly dark olive above with heavy black streaks; ear-patch dark gray; **im + win:** head mostly gray; back olive streaked with black; underparts yellow, only lightly streaked.
• Transient (and summer resident in high mountain coniferous forest); old second-growth, borders, wooded slopes.

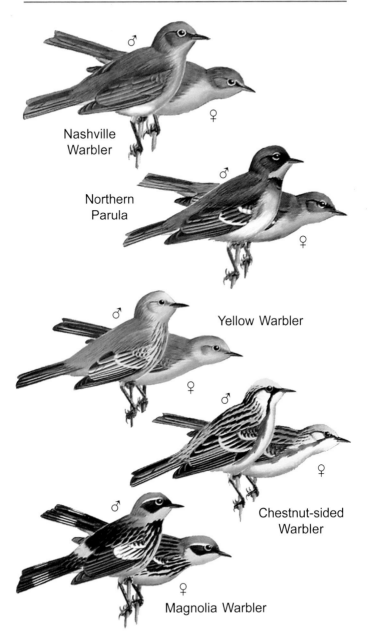

Nashville
Warbler

Northern
Parula

Yellow Warbler

♂

♀

Chestnut-sided
Warbler

♂

♀

Magnolia Warbler

Cape May Warbler   *Dendroica tigrina*

Id: 4.5"; **sum m:** black-streaked olive above, with yellow rump; side of head yellow, with chestnut ear-patch; yellow below with heavy black streaks; **f + win m:** paler and duller; sides of head mostly gray; yellow patch on side of neck; **im:** paler and duller; no yellow except on rump; trace of patch on side of neck.

• Transient; old second-growth, wooded valleys, borders.

Black-throated Blue Warbler   *Dendroica caerulescens*

Id: 5"; white wing-spot; **m:** grayish blue above; black face, throat, and sides; rest of underparts white; **f:** upperparts dark greenish gray to bluish gray; underparts whitish with yellowish tinge; prominent white line over eye; ear-patch blackish.

• Transient (and summer resident at middle and higher elevations); deciduous forest, second-growth, borders.

Yellow-rumped Warbler   *Dendroica coronata*

Id: ("Myrtle" Warbler) **5"**; **sum m:** streaked black and bluish gray above; rump, crown, and side-patch yellow; white line over eye; underparts white except streaky black chest and sides; **sum f:** duller; brownish; streaked above and below; **im + win ad:** duller, less yellow.

• Transient and winter resident; brushy areas, dense hedgerows, borders, woods.

Black-throated Green Warbler   *Dendroica virens*

Id: 4.5"; **sum m:** crown and back unstreaked olive-green; white wing-bars; yellow face, with faint ear-patch; throat (broadly) and sides (streaked) black; breast, belly, and under tail-coverts white; **f + im + win m:** chin and upper throat yellow or whitish; lower throat streaked or blotched with black or gray.

• Transient and summer resident; wooded slopes, borders, second-growth; nests mostly in coniferous forests.

Blackburnian Warbler   *Dendroica fusca*

Id: 5"; **m:** black and white streaked above; orange face, throat, and chest, with black ear-patch; white wing-patch and belly; **f + im:** duller; orange-tinged face, throat, and upper breast; dark ear-patch; whitish scapulars and back-streaks.

• Transient and summer resident; coniferous or mixed forest, upland bogs, open second-growth, borders.

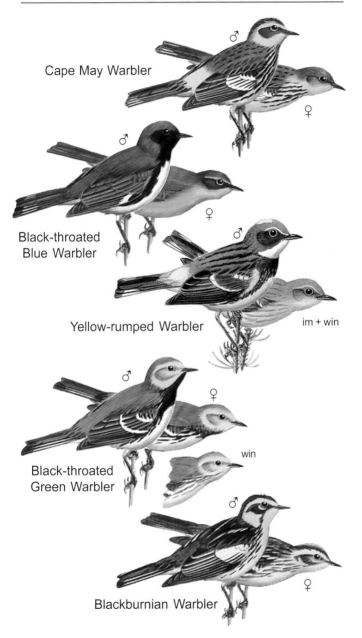

Cape May Warbler

♂

♀

Black-throated
Blue Warbler

♂

♀

Yellow-rumped Warbler

♂

im + win

Black-throated
Green Warbler

♂

♀

win

Blackburnian Warbler

♂

♀

Yellow-throated Warbler   *Dendroica dominica*

Id: 5"; black face-patch; white neck-patch and line over eye; plain gray back; underparts mostly white, but throat and chest yellow, and sides streaked black.
- Transient and summer resident; pine woods, borders, swampy areas, wooded stream valleys.

Pine Warbler   *Dendroica pinus*

Id: 5"; greenish olive above, unstreaked; two white wing-bars; faint line over eye; yellow throat and breast faintly streaked; belly white; **im:** whitish throat and breast.
- Year-round resident, rare in winter; pine forest, patches of pine in mixed second-growth woods.

Prairie Warbler   *Dendroica discolor*

Id: 4.5"; **m:** rufous streaks on greenish above; black-bordered yellow ear-patch; all-yellow below with heavy black side-streaks; **f:** duller; **im:** much duller.
- Transient and summer resident, scrubby woods, borders, overgrown fields, shrubby wet fields.

Palm Warbler   *Dendroica palmarum*

Id: 5"; underparts yellow with rufous streaks on breast and belly; rufous cap; yellowish line over eye; faint wing-bars; rump greenish yellow; bobs tail persistently.
- Transient, and rare winter visitor; on ground, in low shrubs, openings, grassy areas, open shores, clearings.

Bay-breasted Warbler   *Dendroica castanea*

Id: 5"; white wing-bars; black legs; streaked black on brownish or greenish above; belly white; **sum m:** black mask; buff neck-patch; chestnut crown and throat; **f + win m:** whitish throat; only faintly rufous on sides; **im:** faint streaks above, fainter below; under tail-coverts whitish or buff. See immature Blackpoll Warbler.
- Rare transient; borders, hedgerows, wooded stream valleys, old second-growth.

Yellow-throated Warbler

♂ ♀ Pine Warbler

♂ ♀ Prairie Warbler

eastern western Palm Warbler win

win ♂ ♀ Bay-breasted Warbler

Blackpoll Warbler
Dendroica striata

Id 5": white wing-bars; pale legs; **sum m:** streaked black on pale olive above; white below with sides streaked black; black crown; white cheeks and throat; **f + win m:** dark streaks on whitish (below) or dull yellowish green (above); **im:** has whiter under tail-coverts than immature Bay-breasted Warbler, and has *yellowish* legs and feet. See also Black-and-white Warbler.

• Transient; forests, borders, woods, campgrounds, parks.

Cerulean Warbler
Dendroica cerulea

Id: 4.5"; white wing-bars; **m:** blue crown; black streaks on bluish above and on white below; black lower-throat-band; **f + im:** bluish gray or olive-gray above; may be bluer on crown; faint streaks on buffy yellowish below.

• Rare transient, rare and localized summer resident; old-growth deciduous forest, open woods, wooded ravines, borders.

Black-and-white Warbler
Mniotilta varia

Id: 5"; like Blackpoll Warbler, but has streaked or spotted under tail-coverts, **m:** has a white stripe down center of crown; and blackish cheeks; **f:** contrasty black-and-white above and below, *not* finely streaked grayish green on head and back; creeps along tree trunks and large branches.

• Transient and summer resident, and very rare winter visitor; deciduous forest, pine-oak woods, borders, partial clearings.

American Redstart
Setophaga ruticilla

Id: 5"; **ad m:** black with white belly and under tail-coverts; orange patches on sides, wings, and tail; **f:** grayish above; yellow patches on sides, wings, and tail; **im m:** like female but darker, patches more orange.

• Transient and summer resident, mostly below 4000 feet elevation; forest, mixed woodlands, second-growth, borders.

Prothonotary Warbler
Protonotaria citrea

Id: 5.5"; bill black, pointed; **m:** entire head, breast and sides orange-yellow; belly and under tail-coverts white; wings and tail mostly blue-gray; **f:** duller.

• Rare transient, and localized summer resident, mostly near SD and VA BRP; wooded river valleys, wet scrubby woods, swamps, borders.

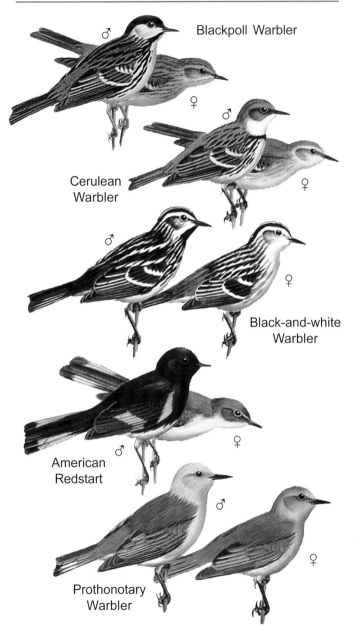

Blackpoll Warbler

♂

♀

♂

Cerulean
Warbler

♀

♂

♀

Black-and-white
Warbler

American
Redstart

♀

♂

♀

Prothonotary
Warbler

97

Worm-eating Warbler   *Helmitheros vermivorum*

Id: 5"; brownish gray above; whitish with buff wash below; head striped black and tawny-buff; bill pointed.

• Transient and summer resident; steep slopes in dense deciduous forest, wooded riversides, wooded ravines.

Swainson's Warbler   *Limnothlypis swainsonii*

Id: 5"; like Worm-eating Warbler, but much paler streak through eye; and crown uniform reddish brown, not striped black-and-buff.

• Rare transient and summer resident; rhododendron thickets, dense forest undergrowth, wooded ravines.

Ovenbird   *Seiurus aurocapilla*

Id: 6"; olive-brown above; broad, black-bordered, orange center-crown-streak; has black streaks on white below; legs pink; tail rather short; usually walks on ground or very low branches.

• Transient and summer resident; forest undergrowth, dense second-growth, wooded slopes.

Northern Waterthrush   *Seiurus noveboracensis*

Id: 6"; like Louisiana Waterthrush, but underparts and line over eye buffy yellowish, *not* white; throat speckled; bobs tail and body as it walks.

• Transient (and very rare summer resident near SD and VA BRP); swamps, wet woods, bogs, borders of ponds and lakes.

Louisiana Waterthrush   *Seiurus motacilla*

Id: 6"; like Ovenbird, with heavy black streaks on white below (but no throat-speckles); but crown plain dark brown, not streaked orange-and-black; bobs tail and body as it walks, often voices a sharp *chip*. See Northern Waterthrush.

• Transient and summer resident; along streams in forest, bogs, wooded lake shores, river banks.

Worm-eating
Warbler

Swainson's
Warbler

Ovenbird

Northern Waterthrush

Louisiana Waterthrush

Kentucky Warbler — *Oporornis formosus*

Id: 5"; **ad:** olive-green above; yellow "spectacles", and long black vertical patch below eye; bright yellow below; **im:** duller; dark patch below eye shorter.

• Transient and summer resident; forest undergrowth, thickets, overgrown clearings; dense second-growth.

Connecticut Warbler — *Oporornis agilis*

Id: 5.7"; like Mourning Warbler, but shows a prominent white eye-ring in all plumages, the under tail-coverts appear longer, and the bird walks rather than hops; **f:** the hood is much browner and less contrasty; **im:** head, throat, and back much browner.

• Rare transient, more likely to be seen in the fall; thickets, overgrown clearings, weedy brushy undergrowth.

Mourning Warbler — *Oporornis philadelphia*

Id: 5.3"; yellowish olive to olive above; yellow below; eye-ring faint or absent; this bird hops rather than walks; **m:** has a distinct medium-gray hood to blackish on chest; **f:** paler hood; **im:** faint hood dull olive.

• Rare transient, more likely to be seen in the spring; brushy borders, undergrowth, thickets.

Common Yellowthroat — *Geothlypis trichas*

Id: 4.5"; **m:** black mask with grayish or white border; underparts yellow, except whitish belly; upperparts medium olive; **f:** no mask; and top and sides of head yellowish green.

• Year-round resident, but rare (and mainly in the lowlands) in winter; around marshy ponds, wet tall-grass meadows, wet thickets.

Kentucky Warbler

im

ad ♂

Connecticut Warbler

ad ♀

Mourning Warbler

♂

♀

♂

Common Yellowthroat

♀

Hooded Warbler   *Wilsonia citrina*

Id: 5.5"; white tail patches; **m:** yellowish olive above; yellow below; yellow face; black hood, including throat; **f:** no hood; olive or blackish crown, yellow throat. See Wilson's Warbler.

• Transient and summer resident; forest undergrowth, borders, partial clearings, ravines.

Wilson's Warbler   *Wilsonia pusilla*

Id: 4.5"; like Hooded Warbler, but has *no* white tail patches, and *no* hood; **m:** has a circular black cap; and yellow, *not* black, sides of neck, and throat; **f:** head and throat all yellow.

• Rare transient; forest, scrubby woods, thickets, borders, lush gardens.

Canada Warbler   *Wilsonia canadensis*

Id: 4.5"; **m:** dark bluish gray above; yellow "spectacles;" yellow below, with white under tail-coverts; black streaky "necklace"; **f + im:** duller; "necklace" faint or absent.

• Transient, and summer resident usually above 3000 feet elevation; forest undergrowth, rhododendron thickets, borders, bogs.

Yellow-breasted Chat   *Icteria virens*

Id: 7"; olive above; white "spectacles;" bright yellow throat and breast; white belly and under tail-coverts; rather thick black bill.

• Transient and summer resident; hedgerows, brushy fields, low shrubby vegetation, overgrown clearings.

♂

♀ Hooded Warbler

Wilson's Warbler

♂

♀

♂

♀ Canada Warbler

Yellow-breasted Chat

Tanagers — Thraupidae

Summer Tanager   *Piranga rubra*

Id: 7"; m: body and head rose-red; wings and tail dark with red feather-edgings; **f + im:** dull grayish yellow below; medium olive above; may be tinged with a patchy reddish wash; wings and tail medium greenish gray.

• Transient and summer resident at lower elevations; deciduous forest, pine woods, borders.

Scarlet Tanager   *Piranga olivacea*

Id: 7"; sum m: scarlet, with black wings and tail; **win m:** like female Summer Tanager, but slightly paler and more olive above and below, and wings and tail *blackish*; **f + im:** like winter male, but wings and tail not as dark (but noticeably more blackish than in female and immature Summer Tanager).

• Transient and summer resident; deciduous forest, old second-growth woods.

Towhees and Sparrows — Emberizidae

Eastern Towhee   *Pipilo erythrophthalmus*

Id: 8"; m: head and sides of neck, and back and wings and tail black (tail has large white corners); breast and belly white; sides and flanks rufous; **f:** like male but brown replaces black.

• Year-round resident; hedgerows, dense borders, undergrowth in deciduous forest, brushy overgrown fields.

American Tree Sparrow   *Spizella arborea*

Id: 6"; streaked above; white wing bars; very pale gray below with black breast spot; crown rufous (feathers tipped whitish); legs blackish.

• SD and BRP. Winter visitor, very rare south of Virginia; overgrown fields, thickets, borders.

Summer Tanager

♂

♀

Scarlet
Tanager

win ♂

♀

sum ♂

Eastern Towhee

♂

♀

American
Tree Sparrow

Chipping Sparrow   *Spizella passerina*

Id: 5.5"; **sum ad:** back heavily streaked; crown rufous, sharply bordered by white line over eye; black line through eye; pale gray nape, cheeks, rump, and underparts; bill black; **im + win ad:** crown fine-streaked; superciliary line and ear-patch brownish gray; bill yellowish.

• Transient, summer resident, and rare winter visitor; grassy fields, borders, hedgerows, residential areas, parks.

Clay-colored Sparrow   *Spizella pallida*

Id: 5"; heavily streaked black on buffy brown back; crown finely black-streaked, with gray center-stripe; nape grayish; ear-patch buff-brown; rump grayish-tan like back-color; whitish below. See winter Chipping Sparrow.

• SD and BRP. Very rare transient and winter visitor; dry grassy fields, overgrown fields, grassy hedgerows.

Field Sparrow   *Spizella pusilla*

Id: 5"; pinkish bill and legs are distinctive; has rufous crown and nape; streaked back and scapulars; white eye-ring and white wing-bars; breast pale grayish buff; amount of rufous wash on sides and flanks variable.

• Year-round resident; weedy fields, grassy overgrown clearings, borders, hedgerows.

Vesper Sparrow   *Pooecetes gramineus*

Id: 6"; streaked above and below with blackish brown; tail notched, with white outer feathers; brownish ear-patch against whitish background; white eye-ring.

• Transient and very rare winter visitor, (and rare summer resident near SD and VA BRP, and northern NC BRP); grassland, grassy borders, pastures, meadows, overgrown fields.

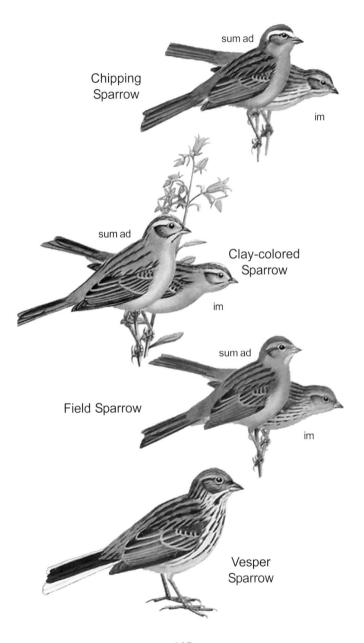

Chipping Sparrow

sum ad

im

sum ad

Clay-colored Sparrow

im

Field Sparrow

sum ad

im

Vesper Sparrow

Lark Sparrow   *Chondestes grammacus*

Id: 6"; entire head striped contrasty black, chestnut, and white; underparts whitish, with black spot on breast; tail rounded; outer tail feathers black, broadly white-cornered; **im:** head much duller; breast streaked.

• Rare and erratic transient and very rare winter visitor; pastures, grassy fields, farmyards, hedgerows, borders.

Savannah Sparrow   *Passerculus sandwichensis*

Id: 5"; streaked above and below; tail notched; generally has yellow above eye.

• Transient, rare winter visitor, and localized summer resident; grassy fields, borders of marshy areas; grassy hedgerows.

Grasshopper Sparrow   *Ammodramus savannarum*

Id: 5"; rich buff throat, breast, sides, and under tail-coverts; crown striped black on buff; back striped black, rufous, and buff; tail short, with pointed feather tips.

• Transient and summer resident; grassy meadows, grassy borders of farm fields, mixed grass, weeds, and low shrubs.

Henslow's Sparrow   *Ammodramus henslowii*

Id: 5"; head and sides of neck grayish olive-green, tawny, and blackish, with a yellowish center streak on crown; streaks on back appear scaly; wings reddish; rump rusty; head looks flat-topped.

• Rare transient (and very rare summer resident near SD and VA BRP); open tall-grass fields, weedy wet meadows.

Nelson's Sharp-tailed Sparrow   *Ammodramus nelsoni*

Id: 5"; crown striped gray and black; line over eye, sides of face and neck, and breast rich buff; underparts otherwise whitish, and only lightly streaked on flanks; back black with narrow white streaks.

• Rare transient; wet meadows, marshy borders of ponds and lakes.

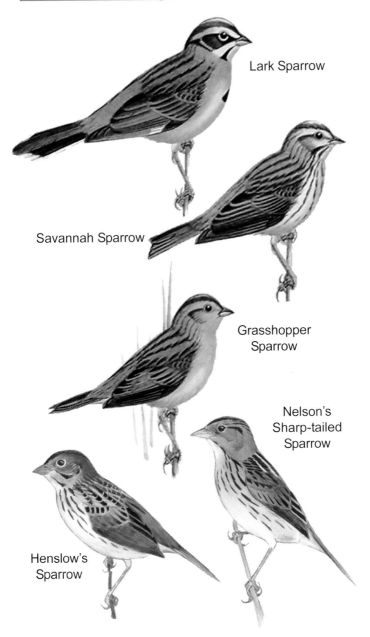

Lark Sparrow

Savannah Sparrow

Grasshopper
Sparrow

Nelson's
Sharp-tailed
Sparrow

Henslow's
Sparrow

Fox Sparrow   *Passerella iliaca*

Id: 6.5"; a large, mainly reddish brown sparrow; crown, nape and back mostly grayish with fine dark reddish brown streaks; rump-patch and tail rufous; underparts whitish with heavy reddish brown, spotty streaks.

• Transient and winter resident; thickets, forest undergrowth and borders, hedgerows.

Song Sparrow   *Melospiza melodia*

Id: 6"; streaked blackish brown on rufos to grayish brown head and back, and on whitish below, with center breast spot; heavy streak on side of throat.

• Year-round resident; gardens, parks, woodland borders, thickets, hedgerows.

Lincoln's Sparrow   *Melospiza lincolnii*

Id: 5"; fine blackish streaks on rich buff breast and sides; lower breast, belly and under tail-coverts white; center crown stripe gray, lateral crown stripes black and reddish brown; sides of face, including line over eye, gray; black-streaked back and scapulars.

• Rare transient; thickets, shrubby borders, hedgerows.

Swamp Sparrow   *Melospiza georgiana*

Id: 5.5"; **sum ad:** streaked brown and black back; wings and rump mostly rufous; center of forehead gray; crown rufous; throat distinctly whitish; chest and sides of head and neck gray; **win ad:** crown finely streaked black, brown, and gray; **im:** ear-patch buffy.

• Transient and winter visitor (and rare and localized summer resident near SD); marshes, wet meadows, overgrown fields, stream valleys.

Fox Sparrow

Song Sparrow

Lincoln's Sparrow

Swamp Sparrow

White-throated Sparrow *Zonotrichia albicollis*

Id: 6.5"; streaked above, ear-patch gray, white wing-bars, white or whitish throat; **two color morphs + intermediates: (1)** head-stripes contrasty black and white; throat contrasty white; bright yellow spot in front of eye; underparts mostly plain pearly gray, or **(2)** head-stripes blackish-brown and dull buff; throat whitish; dull yellowish spot in front of eye; underparts dull brownish gray with darker streaks.

• Transient and winter resident; gardens, thickets, hedgerows, borders, undergrowth.

White-crowned Sparrow *Zonotrichia leucophrys*

Id: 6.5"; **ad:** very contrasty black-and-white crown pattern and line through eye; breast and sides of head and neck pearly gray; throat, belly, and under tail-coverts whitish; bill pinkish or yellowish; back streaked black, brown and whitish; two white wing-bars; **im through first winter:** stripes on crown brown, buff, and whitish.

• Transient and winter resident; thickets, hedgerows, overgrown fields, borders.

Dark-eyed Junco *Junco hyemalis*

Id: 5.5"; **m:** very dark gray all over, except white belly, under tail-coverts, and outer tail feathers; bill pinkish; **f:** may be tinged with brownish on body and head, and tinged with rufous on wings.

• Transient and winter visitor (and year-round resident at higher elevations); borders, thickets, hedgerows, forest, second-growth.

Snow Bunting *Plectrophenax nivalis*

Id: 6.5"; **win:** mostly tawny-buff and white, with black streaks above, and wing-tips broadly black; **sum:** white, with black back, wing-tips, and part of tail.

• Rare and unpredictable winter visitor; short-grass meadows, bare open ridge tops, mountain "balds."

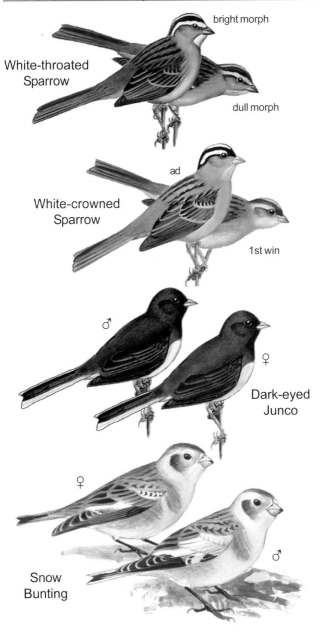

White-throated
Sparrow

bright morph

dull morph

White-crowned
Sparrow

ad

1st win

♂

♀

Dark-eyed
Junco

♀

♂

Snow
Bunting

Cardinals, Grosbeaks, Buntings, and Dickcissel — Cardinalidae

Northern Cardinal   *Cardinalis cardinalis*

Id: 8"; crested; heavy bill red in adult; **m:** bright red all over, except black around base of bill; **f:** grayish-brown and buffy-brown, with red tinge on wings, tail and crest; dark gray around base of bill; **im:** dull dark brown, including bill.

• Year-round resident; scrubby woods, borders, overgrown fields, hedgerows, suburbs.

Rose-breasted Grosbeak   *Pheucticus ludovicianus*

Id: 7.5"; heavy dull yellowish bill; **sum ad m:** black head and back; black-and-white wings and tail; red breast-patch and under wing-coverts; white belly and rump; **win ad m:** much like summer adult male, but duller and browner, streaked and mottled; **f + 1st win m:** streaked dark brown on upperparts, head, and most of underparts; wing-bars and line over eye whitish.

• Transient, and summer resident at middle to higher elevations; deciduous forest, open second-growth, borders.

Blue Grosbeak   *Passerina caerulea*

Id: 6"; bill heavy, contrasty pale grayish; **ad m:** dark violet-blue; with black-streaked back; black wings with rufous wing-bars and feather-edgings; **f:** streaked brownish above; buffy brown below, with some faint streaks; buff wing-bars; rump may be bluish.

• Transient and summer resident, at low elevations; thicke**ts**, open grassy fields, borders, weedy hedgerows.

Indigo Bunting   *Passerina cyanea*

Id: 5"; **sum m:** rich dark blue; **win m:** dark brown above, whitish below; rump and breast tinged blue; **f + im m:** brown above; paler below, faintly streaked. **V:** male often sings from utility wires, or bare high branches — a high-pitched series of double notes and phrases.

• Transient and summer resident; farm fields, roadsides, hedgerows, thickets, borders.

114

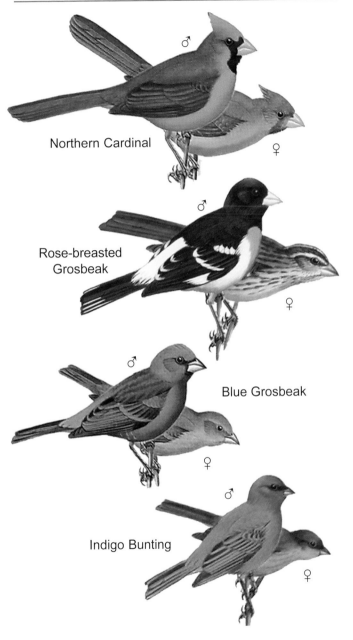

Northern Cardinal

♂

♀

Rose-breasted
Grosbeak

♂

♀

Blue Grosbeak

♂

♀

Indigo Bunting

♂

♀

Dickcissel   *Spiza americana*

Id: 6"; yellowish line over eye; rufous "shoulder" patch; **m:** black or dark gray throat patch; yellow breast; streaked back; **f + im:** much duller; *no* black throat patch; underparts buffy or partly yellow, finely streaked or plain.

• Rare transient and summer resident, and very rare and erratic in winter, mostly near SD and VA BRP; grassy fields, weedy thickets, hedgerows, farm fields.

Blackbirds and Orioles — Icteridae

Bobolink   *Dolichonyx oryzivorus*

Id: 7"; **sum m:** underparts, crown, and sides of head black; scapulars and rump-patch white; nape and hind-neck broadly pale buffy yellow; **f + win m:** like a large buffy sparrow, with dark streaks on buff to tawny buff background, especially on head, back, and flanks; darker above; paler below.

• Transient (and very rare summer resident at higher elevations); hay fields, fields of wheat, oats, or rye, grassy meadows; often in large flocks in migration.

Red-winged Blackbird   *Agelaius phoeniceus*

Id: m – 9", f – 8"; m: black; with red "shoulder" patch which is bordered yellowish or whitish; **f:** dark gray or blackish; heavily streaked below; may show trace of red on wing and pinkish on throat; **im m:** blackish, "scaled" or mottled; "shoulder" patch dull red.

• Year-round resident; marshy areas, moist grassy fields, hay fields and other farm fields; may be in large, single-sex flocks, or mixed flocks, in winter.

Eastern Meadowlark   *Sturnella magna*

Id: 9"; short tail, chunky body; streaked above; mostly bright yellow below, with black breast-patch and side streaks; white outer tail feathers. <u>V</u>: a down-slurred whistle, *chee-wee, chee-wee.*

• Year-round resident, mostly below 3000 feet elevation; grassy fields, unmowed pastures, hay fields.

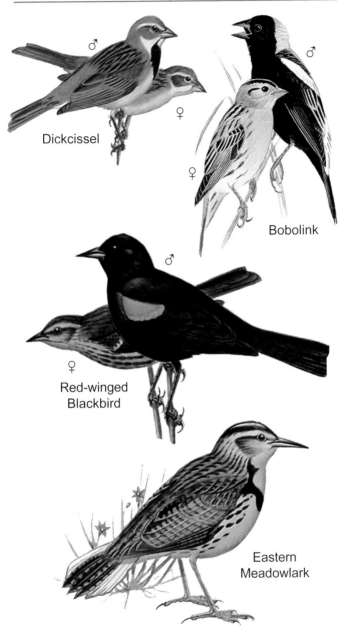

♂

Dickcissel

♀

♂

♀

Bobolink

♂

♀

Red-winged
Blackbird

Eastern
Meadowlark

117

Rusty Blackbird
Euphagus carolinus

Id: 9"; iris pale yellow; tail medium length; **win m:** basically black with pale brownish feather-edgings; **sum m:** black all over, with slight greenish gloss; **f:** paler than male in all plumages.

• Rare transient and winter visitor; farm fields, open woods, hedgerows, borders.

Common Grackle
Quiscalus quiscula

Id: 12"; iris pale yellow; tail rather long; **m:** tail keel-shaped, plumage blackish with purplish or bronzy iridescence; **f:** tail not as noticeably keel-shaped; plumage shows little iridescence.

• Year-round resident, often in large flocks in winter; farm fields, meadows, large gardens and lawns, borders.

Brown-headed Cowbird
Molothrus ater

Id: 7"; **m:** glossy black; except entire head which is dark brown; bill black, short; **f:** dark brownish gray; paler below, and faintly streaked.

• Transient and year-round resident, often in large flocks in winter; farm fields, deciduous forest, partial clearings, borders, hedgerows.

Orchard Oriole
Icterus spurius

Id: 6.5"; **m:** mostly dark reddish brown below, and on rump; entire head to chest, back, and wings (except two wing-bars) black; **f:** greenish olive above; yellowish below; two white wing-bars; **im m:** like female, but throat-to-eye patch black.

• Transient and summer resident, mostly at low elevations; farms, borders, hedgerows, suburbs, open woods.

Baltimore Oriole
Icterus galbula

Id: 7.5"; **m:** mostly bright orange, but entire head and throat, back, and wings (except two wing bars) black; **f:** has two white wing bars, a variable amount of black on head, and is much paler and yellower below; **im:** yellowish gray above; dull yellowish orange below, to whitish belly; two white wing bars.

• Transient and summer resident, and rare winter visitor in parts of our area, mostly below 2000 feet elevation; borders, gardens, parks, farms, along rivers or streams.

win

Rusty Blackbird

sum ♂

sum ♀

♂

♀

im

Common Grackle

♂

♀

Brown-headed
Cowbird

♂

♀

Orchard Oriole

♀

Baltimore
Oriole

♂

Finches and Siskins — Fringillidae

Purple Finch   *Carpodacus purpureus*

Id: 5.5"; **m:** raspberry red, except whitish belly and under tail-coverts, and dark wings and tail; back streaked; head, underparts, and rump faintly streaked; **f:** heavily streaked whitish and dark brownish gray; mustache mark and line over eye whitish; earpatch and streak on side of throat dark brown. See House Finch.

• Irregular transient and winter resident throughout (and rare summer resident in spruce and fir forests at high elevations); coniferous and mixed forest, weedy borders, hedgerows, suburbs.

House Finch   *Carpodacus mexicanus*

Id: 5.5"; **m:** rump, and most of head and breast rosy-red; nape and back brownish gray; streaked above and below; **f:** dull grayish brown, streaked above and below; with dark wings and tail, but no contrasty face streaks. See Purple Finch.

• Year-round resident, mostly below 3500 feet elevation; suburban gardens, mixed farms and overgrown fields, hedgerows, parks, weedy borders.

Red Crossbill   *Loxia curvirostra*

Id: 6"; bill crossed; wings and forked tail black; **ad m:** brick red; **f:** dull yellowish gray; back and crown streaked; **im:** heavily streaked gray, dark above, pale below. <u>V</u>: call in flight a *dip-dip* or *clip-clip*.

Rare and unpredictable transient and year-round resident, mostly above 2500 feet elevation; open pine forest, other coniferous forest, scattered pines on dry rocky ridges.

Common Redpoll   *Carduelis flammea*

Id: 6"; whitish below; streaked on sides and flanks; has white wing bars, red fore-crown, and black lores and chin; **m:** chest rosy-red to pink, streaked on sides and flanks; **f:** some dark streaks on chest and sides; *no* red on underparts.

• Usually very rare transient and winter visitor, but numbers vary greatly from year to year; brushy overgrown fields, woodland borders, open woods, around bird feeders.

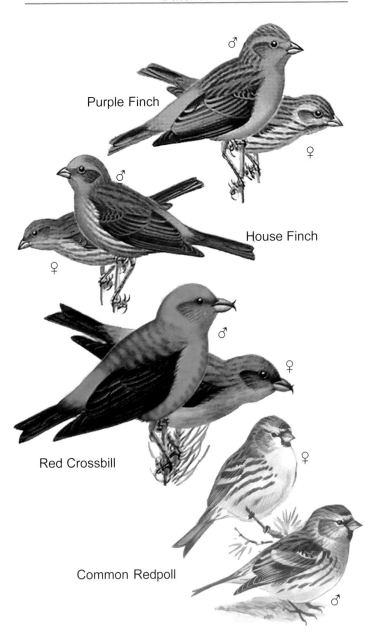

Purple Finch ♂ ♀

House Finch ♂ ♀

Red Crossbill ♂ ♀

Common Redpoll ♀ ♂

Pine Siskin   *Carduelis pinus*

Id: 4.5"; bill small and pointed; **m:** streaked blackish brown on pale grayish brown; yellow patch on forked tail, and yellow stripe on wings; **f:** shows less yellow.

• Year-round resident and winter visitor, may be in flocks in winter, often with goldfinches; numbers vary greatly from year to year; pine, spruce, and fir forests, suburban areas, parks, borders, campgrounds.

American Goldfinch   *Carduelis tristis*

Id: 4.5"; sum m: bright yellow, with black crown patch, wings, and tail; white upper and under tail-coverts; yellowish wrist patch, white wing bar; **f + win m:** mostly olive-green or buffy olive, with whitish belly and under tail-coverts; blackish wings, with white wing bars; no black on crown.

• Year-round resident; borders, hedgerows, weedy overgrown fields, suburban areas, backyard feeders.

Evening Grosbeak   *Coccothraustes vespertinus*

Id: 7"; heavy bill pale greenish or whitish; wings and tail black; **m:** head, chest, and upper back blackish brown with broadly yellow forehead; remaining underparts and upperparts golden yellow; white wing patch; **f:** much duller; and has mostly gray head; no yellow on head.

• Unpredictable winter visitor, usually rare, but numbers may vary greatly from year to year; pine or other conifers, deciduous woods, partial clearings, suburban areas.

House Sparrows — Passeridae

House Sparrow   *Passer domesticus*

Id: 6"; **m:** gray, chestnut and whitish head pattern; throat and chest gray, gradually becoming black as pale gray feather-tips wear off; pale gray breast and belly; streaked black-and-brown back; **f:** mostly brownish gray; streaked blackish and brown above; buffy line over eye.

• Year-round resident, mostly at low elevations; shopping centers, suburban areas, farmyards, parks, campgrounds.

Pine Siskin

American Goldfinch

Evening Grosbeak

House Sparrow

Extremely Rare, Localized, or Casual Species

The following species are not to be expected on most field trips, but they may be seen in our area a few times every five or ten years, or in very small numbers at a few specific localities.

1. Fulvous Whistling-Duck   *Dendrocygna bicolor*

Transient and winter visitor, near SD and VA BRP; plumage tawny below.

2. Greater White-fronted Goose   *Anser albifrons*

Transient and winter visitor, near SD.

3. Cackling Goose   *Branta hutchinsii*

Winter visitor; like Canada Goose, but smaller (25–30"), voice higher-pitched; appears squarer-headed, shorter-billed, shorter-necked. **(Not illustrated)**

4. Mute Swan   *Cygnus olor*

Visitor near SD and VA BRP; bill reddish orange with black knob near base.

5. Eurasian Wigeon   *Anas penelope*

Transient and winter visitor, near SD and VA BRP; white wing patch; **m:** rufous head.

6. Surf Scoter   *Melanitta perspicillata*

Transient and winter visitor, SD and VA BRP; **m:** white nape; **f:** two-spotted face.

7. White-winged Scoter   *Melanitta fusca*

Transient and winter visitor; white wing patch; **f:** two pale face patches.

8. Long-tailed Duck   *Clangula hyemalis*

Transient and winter visitor near SD and VA BRP; **f:** blackish cheek patch.

9. Red-throated Loon   *Gavia stellata*

Transient and winter visitor near SD and BRP; slender bill; **win:** speckled back.

10. Red-necked Grebe   *Podiceps grisegena*

Transient and winter visitor near SD and BRP; **win:** white streak below gray cheeks.

11. Glossy Ibis   *Plegadis falcinellus*

Transient and late-summer visitor near SD and BRP; greenish-glossed purplish brown.

*black-and-white images

12. Wood Stork   *Mycteria americana*

Summer visitor, near SD and BRP; black-and-white wings; black head, bill, and tail.

13. Swallow-tailed Kite   *Elanoides forficatus*

Late summer visitor and fall transient; forked tail; **im:** streaked.

14. Mississippi Kite   *Ictinia mississippiensis*

Transient and summer visitor near VA BRP and in GSM; gray; head pearly.

15. Yellow Rail   *Coturnicops noveboracensis*

Fall transient, near SD and BRP; barred above; buffy face and chest.

16. Black Rail   *Laterallus jamaicensis*

Fall transient, near BRP; mostly dark gray; dark rufous nape patch.

17. Common Moorhen   *Gallinula chloropus*

Spring transient; dark bluish purple; red bill and forehead; white line on side.

18. Sandhill Crane   *Grus canadensis*

Transient; gray with red cap; plumes droop over tail; **im:** brownish, *no* red cap.

19. Red Knot   *Calidris canutus*

Transient near SD and VA BRP; **sum:** reddish brown; **win:** pale gray to whitish.

20. Baird's Sandpiper   *Calidris bairdii*

Transient, near SD and VA BRP; wings extend beyond tail tip; back appears scaly.

21. Long-billed Dowitcher   *Limnodromus scolopaceus*

Fall transient, SD and VA BRP; long bill; alarm call *kleek.*

22. Wilson's Phalarope   *Phalaropus tricolor*

Transient, near SD and VA BRP; **win:** whitish below, pale gray above.

23. Red-necked Phalarope   *Phalaropus lobatus*

Transient near VA BRP; **sum:** rufous "bib" and white throat; **win:** white below; black nape to mid-crown.

24. Red Phalarope   *Phalaropus fulicarius*

Fall transient; heavier bill; **win:** whitish below; black hindneck.

25. Snowy Owl   *Bubo scandiacus*

Winter visitor near SD and BRP; large (23"); round headed, white with few to many black bars and/or spots. (**Not illustrated**)

26. Rufous Hummingbird   *Selasphorus rufus*
Fall to winter visitor (mostly im birds), SD and BRP; note **f** tail pattern.

27. Red-cockaded Woodpecker   *Picoides borealis*
Resident, GSM; barred back; white cheeks; spots below.

28. Western Kingbird   *Tyrannus verticalis*
Late summer and fall transient; medium gray back; yellow belly.

29. Scissor-tailed Flycatcher   *Tyrannus forficatus*
Late spring and summer visitor; **im:** tail shorter than adult's.

30. Northern Shrike   *Lanius excubitor*
Winter visitor, SD and NC BRP; **im:** browner, more heavily barred than adult.

31. Le Conte's Sparrow   *Ammodramus leconteii*
Transient; buffy chest and face; sparsely streaked sides.

32. Harris's Sparrow   *Zonotrichia querula*
Winter visitor; black crown, throat, and eye patch; much less black in winter.

33. Lapland Longspur   *Calcarius lapponicus*
Winter visitor, near SD and BRP; black throat; white tail corners.

34. Painted Bunting   *Passerina ciris*
Visitor, near VA BRP; **f:** mostly a distinctive lime green, paler and yellower below.

35. Yellow-headed Blackbird   *Xanthocephalus xanthocephalus*
Fall and winter; yellow throat and chest; white wing patch.

36. Brewer's Blackbird   *Euphagus cyanocephalus*
Winter visitor; **m:** black, with white eye; **f:** dark brown, dark eye.

37. Pine Grosbeak   *Pinicola enucleator*
Winter visitor; wing bars; swollen bill; **m:** pale red; **f:** medium olive-gray.

38. White-winged Crossbill   *Loxia leucoptera*
Winter visitor, usually in conifers; white wing bars; crossed bill.

Stray or Accidental Species

The following species have been reported in our area only once or twice, or a very few times, in the past fifty years, generally far out of their normal range and usually after severe weather events.

Ross's Goose *Chen rossii.* Near SD.

Brant *Branta bernicla.* Near SD and in GSM.

Harlequin Duck *Histrionicus histrionicus.* Near VA BRP.

Black Scoter *Melanitta nigra.* Near SD.

Eared Grebe *Podiceps nigricollis.* Near SD.

Western Grebe *Aechmophorus occidentalis.* Near SD.

Black-capped Petrel *Pterodroma hasitata.* SD and VA BRP.

White-faced Storm-Petrel *Pelagodroma marina.* SD.

Leach's Storm-Petrel *Oceanodroma leucorhoa.* Near SD.

Band-rumped Storm-Petrel *Oceanodroma castro.* GSM.

White-tailed Tropicbird *Phaethon lepturus.* Near SD.

American White Pelican *Pelecanus erythrorhynchos.* VA BRP.

Brown Pelican *Pelecanus occidentalis.* VA BRP.

Anhinga *Anhinga anhinga.* Near SD.

Greater Flamingo *Phoenicopterus ruber.* Near SD.

Swainson's Hawk *Buteo swainsoni.* Near SD.

Gyrfalcon *Falco rusticolus.* Near SD.

Purple Gallinule *Porphyrio martinica.* SD and VA BRP.

Limpkin *Aramus guarauna.* Near VA BRP.

Piping Plover *Charadrius melodus.* Near VA BRP.

American Avocet *Recurvirostra americana.* Near SD and BRP.

Whimbrel *Numenius phaeopus.* Near BRP.

Hudsonian Godwit *Limosa haemastica.* Near VA BRP.

Marbled Godwit *Limosa fedoa.* Near SD.

Ruff *Philomachus pugnax.* Near VA BRP.

Pomarine Jaeger *Stercorarius pomarinus.* Near VA BRP.

Lesser Black-backed Gull *Larus fuscus.* Near VA BRP.

Glaucous Gull *Larus hyperboreus.* Near SD and VA BRP.

Great Black-backed Gull *Larus marinus.* Near SD.

Gull-billed Tern *Sterna nilotica.* Near VA BRP.

Royal Tern *Sterna maxima.* Near VA BRP.

Sandwich Tern *Sterna sandvicensis.* Near SD.

Roseate Tern *Sterna dougallii.* Near VA BRP.

Least Tern *Sterna antillarum.* Near SD and VA BRP.

Sooty Tern *Sterna fuscata.* Near the VA BRP.

Black Skimmer *Rynchops niger.* Near SD and VA BRP.

Common Ground-Dove *Columbina passerina.* Near BRP.

Groove-billed Ani *Crotophaga sulcirostris.* Near SD.

Green Violet-ear *Colibri thalassinus.* Near NC BRP.

Bewick's Wren *Thryomanes bewickii.* Extinct (?) in our area.

Mountain Bluebird *Sialia currucoides.* Near NC BRP.

Varied Thrush *Ixoreus naevius.* Near VA BRP.

Western Tanager *Piranga ludoviciana.* Near BRP.

Lark Bunting *Calamospiza melanocorys.* Near VA BRP.

Chestnut-collared Longspur *Calcarius ornatus.* Near VA BRP.

Black-headed Grosbeak *Pheucticus melanocephalus.* VA BRP.

Checklist of Birds

Shenandoah National Park, Blue Ridge Parkway, and Great Smoky Mountains National Park

CLASS AVES

Order Anseriformes

Anatidae

Fulvous Whistling-Duck 124c
Greater White-fronted Goose 124c
Snow Goose 10
Ross's Goose 130a
Brant 130a
Cackling Goose 124c
Canada Goose 10
Mute Swan 124
Tundra Swan 10
Wood Duck 10
Gadwall 10
Eurasian Wigeon 124c
American Wigeon 12
American Black Duck 12
Mallard 12
Blue-winged Teal 12
Northern Shoveler 12
Northern Pintail 12
Green-winged Teal 14
Canvasback 14
Redhead 14
Ring-necked Duck 14
Greater Scaup 14
Lesser Scaup 14
Harlequin Duck 130a
Surf Scoter 124c
White-winged Scoter 124c
Black Scoter 130a

a = stray or accidental
c = rare, localized, or casual
ex = may be extinct in our area

Long-tailed Duck 124c
Bufflehead 16
Common Goldeneye 16
Hooded Merganser 16
Common Merganser 16
Red-breasted Merganser 16
Ruddy Duck 16

Order Galliformes

Phasianidae

Ring-necked Pheasant 40
Ruffed Grouse 40
Wild Turkey 40

Odontophoridae

Northern Bobwhite 40

Order Gaviiformes

Gaviidae

Red-throated Loon 124c
Common Loon 18

Order Podicipediformes

Podicipedidae

Pied-billed Grebe 18
Horned Grebe 18
Red-necked Grebe 124c
Eared Grebe 130a
Western Grebe 130a

Order Procellariiformes

Procellariidae

Black-capped Petrel 130a

Hydrobatidae
White-faced Storm-Petrel 130a
Leach's Storm-Petrel 130a
Band-rumped Storm-Petrel 130a

Order Pelecaniformes
Phaethontidae
White-tailed Tropicbird 130a

Pelecanidae
American White Pelican 130a
Brown Pelican 130a

Phalacrocoracidae
Double-crested Cormorant 18

Anhingidae
Anhinga 130a

Order Ciconiiformes
Ardeidae
American Bittern 20
Least Bittern 20
Great Blue Heron 20
Great Egret 20
Snowy Egret 20
Little Blue Heron 22
Tricolored Heron 22
Cattle Egret 22
Green Heron 22
Black-crowned Night-Heron 22
Yellow-crowned Night-Heron 22

Threskiornithidae
White Ibis 24
Glossy Ibis 124c

Ciconiidae
Wood Stork 126c

Cathartidae
Black Vulture 42
Turkey Vulture 42

Order Phoenicopteriformes
Phoenicopteridae
Greater Flamingo 130a

Order Falconiformes
Accipitridae
Osprey 42
Swallow-tailed Kite 126c
Mississippi Kite 126c
Bald Eagle 42
Northern Harrier 44
Sharp-shinned Hawk 44
Cooper's Hawk 44
Northern Goshawk 44
Red-shouldered Hawk 46
Broad-winged Hawk 46
Swainson's Hawk 130a
Red-tailed Hawk 46
Rough-legged Hawk 46
Golden Eagle 48

Falconidae
American Kestrel 48
Merlin 48
Gyrfalcon 130a
Peregrine Falcon 48

Order Gruiformes
Rallidae
Yellow Rail 126c
Black Rail 126c
King Rail 24
Virginia Rail 24
Sora 24
Purple Gallinule 130a
Common Moorhen 126c
American Coot 24

Aramidae
Limpkin 130a

Gruidae
Sandhill Crane 126c

Order Charadriiformes
Charadriidae
Black-bellied Plover 26
American Golden-Plover 26
Semipalmated Plover 26
Piping Plover 130a
Killdeer 26

Recurvirostridae
American Avocet 130a

Scolopacidae
Greater Yellowlegs 28
Lesser Yellowlegs 28
Solitary Sandpiper 28
Willet 28
Spotted Sandpiper 28
Upland Sandpiper 30
Whimbrel 130a
Hudsonian Godwit 131a
Marbled Godwit 131a
Ruddy Turnstone 30
Red Knot 126c
Sanderling 30
Semipalmated Sandpiper 30
Western Sandpiper 30
Least Sandpiper 32
White-rumped Sandpiper 32
Baird's Sandpiper 126c
Pectoral Sandpiper 32
Dunlin 32
Stilt Sandpiper 32
Buff-breasted Sandpiper 34
Ruff 131a
Short-billed Dowitcher 34
Long-billed Dowitcher 126c
Wilson's Snipe 34
American Woodcock 34
Wilson's Phalarope 126c

Red-necked Phalarope 126c
Red Phalarope 126c

Laridae
Pomarine Jaeger 131a
Laughing Gull 36
Bonaparte's Gull 36
Ring-billed Gull 36
Herring Gull 36
Lesser Black-backed Gull 131a
Glaucous Gull 131a
Great Black-backed Gull 131a
Gull-billed Tern 131a
Caspian Tern 38
Royal Tern 131a
Sandwich Tern 131a
Roseate Tern 131a
Common Tern 38
Forster's Tern 38
Least Tern 131a
Sooty Tern 131a
Black Tern 38
Black Skimmer 131a

Order Columbiformes
Columbidae
Rock Pigeon 50
Mourning Dove 50
Common Ground-Dove 131a

Order Cuculiformes
Cuculidae
Black-billed Cuckoo 50
Yellow-billed Cuckoo 50
Groove-billed Ani 131a

Order Strigiformes
Tytonidae
Barn Owl 52

Strigidae
Eastern Screech-Owl 52

Great Horned Owl 52
Snowy Owl 126c
Barred Owl 52
Long-eared Owl 54
Short-eared Owl 54
Northern Saw-whet Owl 54

Order Caprimulgiformes

Caprimulgidae

Common Nighthawk 54
Chuck-will's-widow 56
Whip-poor-will 56

Order Apodiformes

Apodidae

Chimney Swift 56

Trochilidae

Green Violet-ear 131a
Ruby-throated Hummingbird 56
Rufous Hummingbird 128c

Order Coraciiformes

Alcedinidae

Belted Kingfisher 58

Order Piciformes

Picidae

Red-headed Woodpecker 58
Red-bellied Woodpecker 58
Yellow-bellied Sapsucker 58
Downy Woodpecker 60
Hairy Woodpecker 60
Red-cockaded Woodpecker 128c
Northern Flicker 60
Pileated Woodpecker 60

Order Passeriformes

Tyrannidae

Olive-sided Flycatcher 62
Eastern Wood-Pewee 62

Yellow-bellied Flycatcher 62
Acadian Flycatcher 62
Alder Flycatcher 64
Willow Flycatcher 64
Least Flycatcher 64
Eastern Phoebe 64
Great Crested Flycatcher 64
Western Kingbird 128c
Eastern Kingbird 66
Scissor-tailed Flycatcher 128c

Laniidae

Loggerhead Shrike 66
Northern Shrike 128c

Vireonidae

White-eyed Vireo 66
Yellow-throated Vireo 66
Blue-headed Vireo 66
Warbling Vireo 68
Philadelphia Vireo 68
Red-eyed Vireo 68

Corvidae

Blue Jay 68
American Crow 68
Fish Crow 70
Common Raven 70

Alaudidae

Horned Lark 70

Hirundinidae

Purple Martin 70
Tree Swallow 72
Northern Rough-winged Swallow 72
Bank Swallow 72
Cliff Swallow 72
Barn Swallow 72

Paridae

Carolina Chickadee 74
Black-capped Chickadee 74
Tufted Titmouse 74

Sittidae

Red-breasted Nuthatch 76
White-breasted Nuthatch 76
Brown-headed Nuthatch 76

Certhiidae

Brown Creeper 76

Troglodytidae

Carolina Wren 78
Bewick's Wren 131ex
House Wren 78
Winter Wren 78
Sedge Wren 78
Marsh Wren 78

Regulidae

Golden-crowned Kinglet 80
Ruby-crowned Kinglet 80

Sylviidae

Blue-gray Gnatcatcher 80

Turdidae

Eastern Bluebird 80
Mountain Bluebird 131a
Veery 82
Gray-cheeked Thrush 82
Swainson's Thrush 82
Hermit Thrush 82
Wood Thrush 82
American Robin 84
Varied Thrush 131a

Mimidae

Gray Catbird 84
Northern Mockingbird 84
Brown Thrasher 84

Sturnidae

European Starling 86

Motacillidae

American Pipit 86

Bombycillidae

Cedar Waxwing 86

Parulidae

Blue-winged Warbler 88
Golden-winged Warbler 88
Tennessee Warbler 88
Orange-crowned Warbler 88
Nashville Warbler 90
Northern Parula 90
Yellow Warbler 90
Chestnut-sided Warbler 90
Magnolia Warbler 90
Cape May Warbler 92
Black-throated Blue Warbler 92
Yellow-rumped Warbler 92
Black-throated Green Warbler 92
Blackburnian Warbler 92
Yellow-throated Warbler 94
Pine Warbler 94
Prairie Warbler 94
Palm Warbler 94
Bay-breasted Warbler 94
Blackpoll Warbler 96
Cerulean Warbler 96
Black-and-white Warbler 96
American Redstart 96
Prothonotary Warbler 96
Worm-eating Warbler 98
Swainson's Warbler 98
Ovenbird 98
Northern Waterthrush 98
Louisiana Waterthrush 98
Kentucky Warbler 100
Connecticut Warbler 100
Mourning Warbler 100
Common Yellowthroat 100
Hooded Warbler 102
Wilson's Warbler 102
Canada Warbler 102
Yellow-breasted Chat 102

Index

Index